SPICE UP YOUR SOUL

Jenny Cailing Pugh

ISBN: 978-1-5356-1116-9

Contents

Goals, Goals, Goals, and More Goals

January 1, 2017

TODAY IS THE FIRST DAY of the New Year 2017. The idea just occurred to me that I am going to write one article every day, if this is the only thing that I can do to make my life meaningful. A question follows this idea: What am I supposed to write every day? A diary? Yes, it is a diary of a sorts, but a diary contains the everyday events of my life. What I would like to write every day may be a diary, but the difference would be that I am going to write about my future in the here-and-now setting. It's like I am writing my future day-to-day life as if I am living it today. Could this be possible? I will find out once I start doing it. But what about my goals?

This is actually what I want to write about: goals, goals, goals, and more goals. I want to organize my goals from the smallest to the ultimate goals until one manifests. What is my ultimate goal? To be rich. "I, Jenny, am rich, well, and happy. You, Jenny, are rich, well, and happy. She, Jenny, is rich, well, and happy." I am now going to elaborate on this goal, which is in the form of affirmation.

Rich

What do I mean when I say I am rich? Rich to me means I have an infinite source and supply of money to spend on everything that makes me happy, tangible or intangible. I would like to see myself happily sharing my blessings first to my loved ones, children, grandchildren, brother, sisters, mother, other relatives, and the needy in my horizon. Then I want to spend my money to establish some sort of institution to train and educate people concerning awareness of their true reality. I also want to see myself traveling and doing research on things that interest me, particularly nature, photography, cultures, and the beauty of life. I would also spend my money on those objects that I would like to possess for beauty and comfort, such as a beautiful and spacious home for me and my family. What do I mean when I say I am well?

Well

Wellness to me means I am healthy physically, emotionally, and spiritually. This would be one of the most important areas where I'd spend money. Health, beauty, and talent. I am very good at what I do for the good of all concerned.

Happy

This means that I am happy because I am living as my true self and am capable of doing and having everything I desire.

Okay, so how am I going to achieve all these? The idea is, the universe has infinite ways to manifest all my desires in perfect timing. I am unfolding every day and getting better and better. I may not know how all these desires will manifest, and I don't intend on making mistakes, but I entrust all my desires to God and the universe to bring all my desires to material manifestation.

So what can I write every day beginning today, throughout the year, that would be 365 articles at the end of the year?

The goal is to write one article every day about goals. I did this before in a notebook and it was fun.

I believe this will allow things to manifest for me easily and effortlessly in very satisfactory and harmonious ways. So be it, so it is

Highlights of My Life in 2016

January 2, 2017

EVERY YEAR HAS HIGHLIGHTS IN our lives. There are blessings in our lives that we should value. Life is movement. There may have been some heartaches, disappointments, and failures in the past, but the fact that we are still alive and enjoying the present life only means that we have surpassed all those negative influences and we are moving forward. Moving forward with a determined direction is different than just drifting in life and being carried away without definite direction. Hence, counting our blessings in the past is fundamental to knowing where the direction of our lives is leading. Let's drop those painful memories in the past that hurt and remember them only when those heartaches make us better people in our present. Cherish those memories that make us feel good and that brought us blessings in our present, so that we can carry them toward a bright future.

At the onset of 2016, I joined with my son and his family celebrating the New Year. It was such a happy reunion and one of those rare times that my son and I were reunited in an important celebration of the living. Such bonding time was followed by more and more reunions with the family for various occasions, such as birthdays of the young ones and my *despedida* (a farewell party)

Another memorable time was in January when I received the documents of my corrected birth certificate that had been in process during the whole year of 2015. This triggered me to proceed processing the rest of my necessary documents to come to the United States. The rest is history. This memorable moment boosted my core belief that when the perfect time comes, everything we desire comes to us swiftly and easily.

The best things that happened to me in 2016 can be enumerated as follows: 1) the straightening of all my necessary documents, which took me on some adventures with both government and private offices. Some caused me some anxieties, but now that they are in the past and I have succeeded in my objective. I can only count them as blessings in my life; 2) the constant reunion and celebration in my family, like the summer we spent swimming and the picnics in resorts with the whole family during my eldest granddaughter's graduation in architecture; 3) the birth of my wonderful grandson followed by the monthly celebration of his birth; 4) my coming to the United States to join my husband after five long years of being apart. This was my husband's and my third marriage, which was performed in the United States. This happened simultaneously with me receiving my green card, which would last for ten years.

This was one of those years in my life where God's blessings were manifested according to the desires of my heart. It was such a great year to me. Now, it's 2017 and I have more expectations for this year to bring me and my family and loved ones more blessings. Life is wonderful when all our good intentions and expectations come to us in perfect timing.

Life Is Movement

January 3, 2017

EVERYTHING IN LIFE IS MOVEMENT in all directions and in various speeds and phases of development. Everyone evolves in physical, emotional, spiritual, and knowledge-based ways. Some of the areas in our lives just move on whether we like it or not. To cite one example, physical growth is inevitable for anyone born, whether in the animal or plant kingdom. Change and evolution is a way of life, but then as responsible humans we take charge on nurturing our personal being in order to evolve into somebody who is an asset to society and to achieve the purpose of one's individual life. We have to pay attention to our physical health by eating the right food and doing physical activities for a balance and healthy physical growth. We also have to feed our minds with useful knowledge that we can use as tools to make our socioeconomic life meaningful, not only for ourselves but for the good of everyone concerned. Most of all we have to nourish our spiritual lives because it is the vehicle that transports us from one condition or situation to the next level in the process of our personal evolution.

Growth, development, change, and progress are evidences of a fulfilling life. In every person's heart and mind there is a vacuum that needs to be filled. We humans are born complete with potentials to achieve, but we all need to discover what it is that we want to achieve in order to become a blessing, first to ourselves and then to our loved ones and to all concerned. To satisfy this painful longing in the soul, people resort to various behaviors and activities they consider the best way to achieve it. The process of development is actually the path of happiness. While there is movement in the process of development of one's life, there is also a time for inertia where one has to slow down to listen and to be aware of what his soul is whispering in his heart. Knowledge is limited because each person only knows and understands what he had personally experienced. There is an infinite knowledge in the universe that one person cannot experience, even if he spends his whole life trying to learn all the knowledge in this vast universe. Hence, to use and exhaust all of one's knowledge is not adequate to solve a personal problem or to achieve one's goal in order to succeed.

It is important for a person to consult his soul, the all-knowing soul who knows where you had been, where you are right now, and where you are headed in this journey called life. Whether we do something or nothing, whether we plan or not, and whether we create goals or not, life continues to move on. Whether lifes moves on to fulfillment or to miserable failures depends so much on how we manage our personal lives and on our awareness of the direction of movement and mobility in our lives. This kind of awareness needs some power beyond comprehension of a fallible mind; this is the power of guidance that is supposedly inherent in every human if we just learn how to listen to it. That's why the Bible says in Proverbs 16:25 KJV, "There is a way that seems right unto a man but the end thereof is destruction." This means that we tend to create and do things we think will fill the vacuum, only to find out in the end that we are still unhappy at the least. This is because we fail to consult the all-knowing soul within us. We ignore or are completely unaware of its role and power to guide us on the right path of our journey leading to the perfect destiny, on the individual level. Therefore, the most important and the wisest thing to do is to learn to listen to the voice within and make it your expertise before you start learning the knowledge that is available in your environment. We ignore or are completely unaware of its role and power to guide us on the right path of our journey leading to the perfect destiny, on the individual level. Therefore, the most important and the wisest thing to do is to learn to listen to the voice within and make it your expertise before you start learning the knowledge that is available in your environment.

Emotions: The Transportation
of Our Life's Destiny

January 4,2017

IN THE EARLY TIMES OF human evolution, transportation to move from point A to point B and so on was not as fast and comfortable as it is today. Some curious minds wondered why birds could fly and could easily soar up high in the sky. Others wondered how to cross the ocean and what life could be like across the oceans. This type of curiosity inherent in the minds of human beings led people to invent the airplane and ships. For any distant movement, an effective, comfortable, and efficient vehicle is necessary to transport us to the heights and peaks of our destinations.

Human emotions trigger human beings to think, design, create, and produce objects that can give them, and the rest of humanity, comfort in living. Emotions also cause people to initiate relationships with other people, objects, animals, and even with certain intangible things found only within the secret chambers of human existence. Everything that a person possesses is related to his emotional state. Relationships are not only with other humans; they are also with other animals, places, events, objects, material possessions, and between the physical and the spiritual aspects of a person. A person's quality of life in terms of failure or success in his family relationships, occupational-social and economic status, marital condition, financial, and other material possessions are determined by the quality of emotions he keeps, and he maneuvers to transport all these goods in life toward his direction. Emotions bring us luck or misfortune depending on its quality. The saying "love begets love" is an example of this. If you love a person, he/she will love you in return. If you hate a person, he/she will return such hatred to you. If you love money, money will come to you in great abundance. If you love your pets, your pets will love you and be loyal to you. If you love your job or career, such will find its way to your doorstep and live with you happily ever after and will give you a good reputation for as long as you live. If you love yourself, other people will follow. You become a loving and lovable person, and the list could go on and on.

Everything in life is defined by a certain quality and degree of relationship you maintain with other existing things, humans, inanimate objects, or intangible reality. The quality of relationships you maintain is dependent on what kind of emotions you maneuver to transport those desirable things toward or away from you. Negative emotions are repellent, so they would strip you of all the good things in life. Such life would exist in misery with broken marriages or love relationships, broken family, joblessness, failing an important examination in education or as a job requirement, being broke or other financial difficulties, homelessness, becoming physically weak, haggard, sick, and ugly, and so forth. Theses are just few of life's miserable conditions caused by negative emotions. The important question then is, what is the quality of emotions that perennially lingers within me? You can also check it by evaluating the quality of your life in certain areas. Ask yourself: Do I often experience lack of money? How is my health? Am I beautiful? What are people's comments about my looks? Do my children love me? Is my husband loyal to me? And so forth and so on. Whatever personal diagnosis you discover within you, be thankful and pat your shoulders for the good ones. If they are painfully hurting your feelings and life, for God's sake repair them and set them straight for your own good and for the good of all concerned. You have the power and ability to make your life beautiful. Do it. So be it, so it is.

Dominating Thoughts and Perennial Emotions to Make Your Dreams Come True

January 5, 2017

THOUGHTS ARE THINGS. EVERY MATERIAL thing that exists in this world started in the mind. A person who owns a beautiful house with detailed beauty and functionality started all the possession and creation of such property in his mind. Before actually moving into that house, he already had planned and saw in his mind the details of everything and himself with his family moving into that particular design and location of that house. It's only a matter of perfect timing for him to have manifested such actuality. Now I am dealing with the contents of the mind and the emotions that trigger those contents. One maintains within him in relation to such contents on a day-to-day basis. The mind is the workshop and laboratory of everything that comes and happens in every person's life which means that everything that comes into being or that materialized in a person's life had been done already in his mind, he already had seen and had worked it out clearly in his mind. But first there is the emotion, the emotion or the passion he exerts while he does those things within his mind because it is the passion that carry out those things that he had imagined to become or to do or to have in his material reality.

Everyone wants to live happily in abundance and success—abundance in money, abundance in material possessions, abundance in love, and everything beautiful materially and intrinsically. But why is it that many people say they are only up to dreaming and wishing but nothing has happened to their dreams? Why are they still wallowing in difficulty and lack? I had a good talk with a certain person who said to me, "You are lucky, Jean, because whatever you want comes to you exactly as you want, but I am very unfortunate." Then she started to enumerate her misfortunes and all the lacks and failures and disappointments she could muster. She was excellent in enumerating all her misfortunes, but even if I could see a lot of blessings that happened in her life, she did not see them. She chose all the so-called disappointments to dominate her thoughts and control her emotions.

The following are examples of the stages leading to manifesting a dream or a failure. Stage 1: A desire is born caused by perceived needs or lack in one's life. To cite a situation, perceived lack is triggered when a person sees one of her peers possessing something she finds desirable. Various inner reactions could happen, such as feelings of envy and jealousy. These feelings are negative per se, but they can be turned into positive ones. Instead of bitterness, envy, and jealousy, she could assure herself that she can have those things too because she is able and capable to have them. If a person is positive, she will start to dream and fantasize in details, seeing in her mind that she is in a situation better than the person she envies. Her dominating thoughts might be: "Everything comes to me easily and effortlessly in very harmonious ways for the good of all concerned." Then she could feel happy and enjoy the possibility of making her dreams come true. To make herself happy just by thinking of those good things that could come to her is actually triggering her psyche to make a way for her dreams to manifest. She does not pay attention to the how because it would be beyond her. On the other hand, the bitterness, envy, and jealousy that works in a person's being would make her feel frustrated and unlucky, causing her to start to think of excuses like: "Well, she is lucky because in truth she is younger, prettier, and smarter than me. I am just born unlucky in life, and it's the fault of my parents or God that He made me like this. My family is poor so no matter what I do I just cannot be better than what I am and have now." She would then have the dominating thoughts in her everyday life that she is trying to do her best but there's just nothing and nobody, not even God, who could help her improve her situation. She would wonder if the goddess of fortune would visit her one day, only to cement in her mind and emotions the disbelief and disappointments when she only saw what never changed.

Stage 2: Once a desire to improve one's life is born—due to what she sees and believes to be the good life that she should have—a positive dreamer will start to feel good about herself and her life, thanking God and herself for the mere privilege of being alive. She would start to imagine and collect pictures and objects that are simulations to the situation of her life. Once the dream happens in material reality, she make drawings or a collage of this reality, the reality that only exists in her mind and heart. Her mind's work during the day and at night is to remember all those good fantasies she has dreamed and created in her mind, and no matter what the actual situation at present, her joy is to remember the details of her good life that exist only within her. If her dream is to be rich, then she would imagine how she would look being rich. She will tell herself that she is rich and can afford to buy beautiful clothes for herself, that she can afford to dine in expensive restaurants and eat expensive food. This kind of thinking is a kind of magic. One of the results would be some friends in the past show up and invite her for the sake of the "good ol' days" to dine with her in a special and expensive restaurant, and that she will be the one to pay.

Many more changes and beautiful incidents in your life would happen according to the dominating thoughts and perennial emotions you maintain. This is called "dance of the universe" according to the quality of energy you maintain within you that resonates to the outward reality of your life. On the other hand, take a look at the negative mentality. This person knows all the difficulty she experienced in her life and becomes callous to her desires. She knows that her husband is cheating on her, so she hates him and imagines him having sex with other women. She also knows that her life is deprived of money so her mind goes says, " I don't have enough money for everything. I have no money to pay the bills, the rent, and more needs, but there is not enough money to pay them." She has even suppressed her desire to go to the beauty parlor or buy some new clothes. For her it's ridiculous when she has not even enough money for the basic necessities. Her mind dwells on the debts and payables, and she gets angry for having a life like this. She's not happy in her job and dislikes everybody there. Her dominating thoughts and perennial emotions are complaints, complaints, and remorse. What do you think happens to the life of this type of mind? What happens is creditors will flock to her for the money she owes, she will be fired, her marriage broken, and so forth, because she is perpetuating all the difficulties in her life by constantly making them the dominating thoughts and welcoming them as perennial residents in her emotions. See how important it is to check on the dominating thoughts and the perennial emotions we keep within us? If you have any questions on this topic, I welcome your questions.

Faith that Works as Opposed to Work that Proves Faith

January 6, 2017

CONSIDER THIS IRONY. DOING SOMETHING halfhearted—meaning you don't really believe in the deepest sense for sure that what you do will lead you to achieve your goals—versus truly believing in the deepest sense that you are a success in everything you do even before you start it.

To illustrate my point, I will talk about two people with opposing personalities and principles in life. What they have in common is they have a goal to improve their lives in all areas. Let's call them Tammy and Connie. Tammy realized one day that her life was difficult financially. She liked nice clothes and wanted to look good, but she had no money to buy those things. So she started to dream of going to college, finishing a degree, and then getting a well-paying job so that she could buy what she wanted. But before she could even continue dreaming, something in her mind said, "How can you study in college? Your family is poor, your father has no permanent income, your parents always fight, especially when the children are hungry, and there is nothing to eat." Because of this situation in her family, she forgot dreaming about going to college. Instead, she looked around to find any job that could make her earn some cash to help her family. She just had to forget her desire to look good in those fancy dresses. She said to herself, "It can wait."

She found a job as a saleslady in a small garment store. She started helping her family and saving a little money because she planned to start a small business. She did everything so she could experience a good life. Eventually she was able to start a sar-isari store(a sari-sari store is a smaller version of a convenient store prevalent in the Philippines) because she was able to get a loan.

A few months had passed, and the business was not as good as she thought it would be. It failed to give her the income that she should have calculated as she was starting. She was discouraged. She thought that there was nothing anymore that she could do to improve her life condition. Her faith in her dreams, in her plans, in herself, and in life as a whole had vanished. She had accepted herself as a failure, unlucky in life. So she just let her life drift by until one day she saw a neighbor, a childhood friend who became her lover and they married. He was also jobless. She perpetuated her life of failure by losing her faith in every good thing that she could possibly have. If only her faith in life was strong.

On the opposite side, let's talk about Connie. Connie also came from a very poor family. Like Tammy, her parents also fought and her father was a jobless drunk. Her siblings were always hungry, but she had ambitions. She wanted to save her family from poverty, and she believed she could do it because she was the eldest and beautiful. Like Tammy, she wanted to have nice clothes and other things. She believed she could have everything she wanted in life. She had that kind of feeling, but she had no idea how it was going to happen. She just believed in herself, had a deep feeling that she deserved everything good in life, and that it would all come to her in the perfect time.

One day one of her friends told her that they both would apply as a sales clerks in a garment store. She thought about it and decided that that was not what she wanted to do; she didn't want to be a servant of anyone else. Her friend got the job and Connie was jobless. She believed that the right job for her would present itself if she knew what she really wanted to do. At home, Connie realized that she liked to do crochet work. She loved creating designs and producing beautiful crochet work. One day her aunt came by and brought some threads for crochet. Connie was curious and happy seeing them, and in their conversation she had expressed to her aunt that she loved doing crochet. From then on, her aunt would buy her threads so that Connie was able to finish a lot of crochet products. Her aunt had a business in distributing crochet products to wholesale dealers. Connie found her niche in life; she had learned the business until she became the manager of her aunt's business. Eventually, she also became the owner of a business similar to her aunt's in another town. She had studied the potential of the business and the operation system. She was an entrepreneur and eventually became wealthy, just by doing what she really wanted to do and putting all her energies into it.

Lessons from the two stories: Tammy had ambition, but she had no originality. She just drifted in life chasing rainbows. There was no concrete direction in her dreams. Connie believed in herself and rejected anything that didn't contribute to her deepest desires. Let faith work for you instead of working harder in order to prove your faith in yourself.

Money Relationship

January 7, 2017

LIKE I SAID IN MY previous articles, relationships are not just with other humans or other living things but also with inanimate objects. This time I will give insights on money relationship.

Anywhere in the world money is always an issue to be concerned about. Economics is very much about the study of allocating scarce resources, production, income, and distribution of wealth. When we talk of money, what comes into your mind? When we talk of problems in any areas of life, what comes into your mind as an instant solution? How many times have you heard statements such as "If only I had plenty of money, I could have done this, or could have possessed that, or would have no problem in this..." Money is energy, meaning it is powerful in many, if not most or all, of life's activities and functions. Who would say he does not need or like money in all truthfulness and honesty? Money may not be everything in life, but admittedly it can do a lot if not most of everything that makes life functional and more meaningful. Whether you agree or not the fact remains that money has a big role in most areas in life.

Once upon a time, barter trade was the game. A farmer would barter his products with products he needed that cannot be produced on the farm, such as clothes, shoes, salt, and more. Money makes things easier, more beautiful, and comfortable in life. But why do so many people feel and experience a lack of money? Why would many people feel like there's not enough money to go around? The direct answer to this is in the quality of relationship one has with money. The questions would be: How is your relationship with money? Do you respect, trust, and believe in it as part of yourself? Try to investigate yourself concerning your relationship with your family members, lover, or spouse. What makes your relationship with them harmonious? What makes you stick together for better or for worse? Can you make a parallel to your relationship with money? This I can safely say. If you want money to keep coming to you, and for it to stick with you for better or for worse, establish a durable and lasting relationship with it by trusting it to come to you. Love money for its real value in your life. Don't say bad words about it. Love it like you love yourself, your family, and your loved ones. Treat it with respect and honesty. You may not need to worship and adore it because you won't be sincere by doing that, but just treat it like it deserves respect. Don't chase money. If you do money will flee away from you. Where could you find anything when chased would also meet you to be captured or punished? Let money come to you by saying to yourself with deep faith, understanding, and trust, "Money, come to me easily and effortlessly in floods of abundance and in perfect harmony for the highest good of all concerned." This statement is a standard affirmation to yourself that you do regularly in a given period, most commonly for 28 days, in writing or spoken quietly or aloud until your subconscious mind will accept it as true then watch how your financial life change for the better.

Don't say to yourself that it is hard to find money. By doing that you are just perpetuating your belief that money is hard to get and you will live in lack. And if money is already in your hands, you will just waste it and it will suddenly go. The point here is to establish a healthy and durable relationship with money. You will never fail if you do. You will never experience lack. Believe me.

The Issue of Manifestation

January 8, 2017

EVERYBODY WANTS TO SUCCEED IN life such that they believe that they have to work hard and exhaust themselves to the limit, if not even beyond their limits, in order to succeed and to make their dreams come true. There are two principles that I would like to present here in the issue of manifestation. Manifestation means making your dreams come true or achieving your goals. The two concepts are: 1) going with the flow and 2) chasing rainbows. Both of these principles need personal efforts, but one is a sure method to succeed while the other is a sure method to fail. The choice is yours. But first I would like to differentiate the two concepts.

Going with the flow is like making success in life easily, more relaxed than exerting so much effort and pushing yourself very hard to get what you want in life. Imagine you are floating downstream in a river. If you allow yourself to be carried downstream by the current of the river, while being alert to sway here and there a little to evade rocks and boulders, you will definitely reach the sea safely without exhausting so much effort. Hence, there is no waste of energy, but the direction is sure and you would arrive in perfect timing with less effort. That is the best illustration of the concept of going with the flow.

On the other hand, chasing rainbows means running round and round while looking up at the unreachable rainbow in the sky, but you just run in circles without accomplishing anything. All you do is stumble and bruise yourself.

In making improvements in our lives, and even in solving difficult situations, we have these two methods from which we have to choose. Just one, the concept of going with the flow, is a sure method of achieving goals easily and effortlessly in perfect timing. Chasing rainbows is a trial and error that takes forever, a tedious waste of energy that surely ends in failure because the rainbow is in the sky. It may be wonderful to behold and dream of, but it is beyond human reach. Going with the flow is attracting those things you dream of—attract money, attract the good life that you desire, attract to you everything that you would like to manifest to make your life meaningful and full of happiness. Make yourself a magnet of everything you want to be, do, and possess. Be the master of those things you desire rather than being the slave of those things you dream of. You should learn how to become the magnet and master of those things you desire and how to make them happen effortlessly according to your wishes. Remember that everything you dream of is energy.

Energy is power; hence, those things you dream of are power because they energize you. Money is energy because it empowers you. It gives you power and ability to do what you want to do, buy what you want to buy, and go places you could not go without the power of money. It also helps you to maintain health and beauty. To have plenty of money is not to become its slave like you work hard for it so that money will be pleased and you can have plenty of it. Remember, you are just a slave and a slave will get nothing or very little. Whereas if you are the master of money, money will race toward you and flow in your direction in infinite abundance. If your mind says, "How could I have plenty of money?" Somewhere within you, the logical mind will provide you answers that are only according to its limited knowledge. It may give you answers such as "Get a job and work hard" or "build a business and be good in it." You may try doing what your logical mind is suggesting to you. In this sense, you will get nothing of what you dream of or, you just get a little money, enough to live by. Most often it's not even enough. To be the master of money you have to be more powerful than money. Like attracts like. When money senses that you are full of energy and powerful it will suddenly incline to your direction. Money will make you its master so that more and more money will join forces to add to your energy then you will become more and more powerful.

So far you have just read theory. Many times a theory is difficult to understand because there are always opposing theories within us, as influenced by our experiences and what we heard from parents, teachers, and our religious upbringing. There might be many questions within you such as: Does this mean I don't have to work? Should I just wait for a fairy godmother or the goddess of fortune to drop down from nowhere to bring me all the money I wanted to possess? Don't be ridiculous. I am not talking impossible things here. I am talking about scientific methods in physics, gravity, and how energy works; these are laws of the universe. Your question should be, how can I become the master of money or of anything that I desire to become, do, and possess? That should be the most sensible and wisest question you ask yourself so that you will unfold and evolve until something within you eventually gives you the right answer. Once you get the perfect answer, then that is the time you start putting effort toward your goal. A kind of effort that is easy like swaying here and there to evade boulders until you become the person you really are intended to be, hence, deserving of everything that is rightfully yours since time immemorial.

Manifestation is a deep study that needs the space of a whole book. Any of you who would like to know more about this subject, feel free to ask me on my site jennypughlife.com. Good luck and God bless.

Master of Your Own Life

January 9, 2017

THE ADAGE "LIFE IS WHAT you make it" has a very important message to ponder. I would like to add: "I am the master of my own fate" and "We are the creators of our own luck." Many times I heard people say: "I am just not as lucky as you are, Jean." Some friends have told me that they did what I had been doing in my life, but they just did not get so lucky regarding love in marriage, family, children, position in the job, and education. A friend of mine said that she saw me as being lucky ever since we first met. She said that I was always lucky in everything that I did because according to her I am stubborn, daring, and brave. See what I mean with "we are the creators of our own luck"? Stubborn, daring, and brave are inner qualities and power that invite luck and manifest it in our lives. I don't believe in sheer luck. If there is any luck at all, you should have invited that into your life without you even knowing it. It's your mental attitude, the energy in your mind, that accidentally invited the so-called luck to drop by in your life. But notice that many of those who have stumbled on sheer luck through gambling lost the money sooner than they got it through "good luck." It did not stay long because the so-called luck just dropped by. But once it realizes that you don't deserve it, it will quickly jump out the window of your soul and life.

It reminds me of a Filipino taxi driver who won 40 million pesos, (an equivalent of $800,00 in the currency rate of P50 to a dollar). It is a large amount of money for a person who never had a lot of money in his life before. He thought that such an amount was infinite and life changing, that no matter how he spent it would not run out. Within that year he bought a condominium unit worth 15 million pesos ($300,000) in the heart of Manila. He also bought twenty units of taxi cabs thinking that he would have a stable income in the future from renting out those taxi cabs. There is nothing wrong in acquiring and possessing these things. What made it wrong was he started to live a life that would throw away all that he got. He let his friends drive his taxi cabs and did not ask for the rent because his objective was to help those poor taxi drivers. Then his relatives who visited him increased in number. Each had major financial needs, such as wedding expenses for one, and another was going to study college and asked him to finance him. Some wanted to build houses because they were homeless. Another asked for capital in a small business that he contemplated to start. More and more relatives, friends, and even those he never met before became his relatives and friends for his "good luck" money. He was overjoyed by his money. It made him feel powerful by giving away his money and spending it without limits.

He started going out for fun and pleasure every night to the point that his wife and family were disappointed because he was giving away money to excessive drinking with "friends" and prostituting. He rarely went home to his wife and family; he was just overwhelmed by his new fortunate life. As a result, all his money was gone in the same year. The taxi cabs needed repair and he had no more money to spend for that, so he sold his condominium and all his taxi cabs eventually. In the end, he lost everything including his marriage and family, his "friends" and "relatives," and he went back to his old job as a taxi driver. Then he said to himself, "I am just born as a taxi driver and cannot be otherwise."

Being the master of your own life means that you are foremost for yourself no matter what. If you won't stand by yourself, who will? And if you are for yourself, love yourself above all. Loving yourself means knowing what you need before knowing the needs of others. You will be disappointed in life if you will give away everything you have hoping that one day they will give you back what good you had given them. It does not work that way. Do some introspection and survey the contents of your heart and mind at all times.

Celebrating Life

January 10, 2017

JANUARY 10, 1955 WAS THE day I was born and the beginning of a life to celebrate. Sixty-two years ago there was chaos in my father's household. After twenty-one years of marriage that did not bear a child of their own, my mom and dad finally had a baby; it was me. But there was a twist. My mom was not my biological mother; it was Esperanza, a young woman twenty-six years old, while my dad was forty-seven. Regardless of the circumstances of my birth, I still praise God to have created me and given me this wonderful life.

When I was just sixteen I created a short poem that has become my principle in life since then. Here are some lines I extracted from it:

This humble life of mine is given to me by God;
I will make use of this to make the giver Glad.
Life is like a flower it blossoms at the start of the day
and it fades at the end of the day.

I now know the purpose of my life, and it's not just my birthday that I am going to celebrate. I thank my biological mother, my father, and my mom to have been the channel used by God to make my life on earth possible. But I thank my God most of all because He has always been with me in all the steps I have decided to tread. Life is a celebration when God is always with and within us. I have a pact with my Lord in heaven that in everything I do I will always glorify Him in my life in any way I can. In glorifying my Father in heaven, I am willing to do His will as He guides me in all my life's journey.

In the sixty-two years that I have lived this life, there have been lots of twists and turns, but I always feel God's presence in my life whether I am on my peak or in my lowest times. My fervent prayer to my God is to let me be a channel of blessings to everyone I have contact with. I want everyone on my horizon to celebrate life with me in all situations and conditions. My objective is to let everyone know and use the gifts that God has given to each of those who He died for. Friends, you are precious. We are all precious in the heart of God. Let's celebrate life to the fullest.

Maintaining Self-Value

January 11, 2017

EVERY HUMAN BORN IN THIS life is a winner in his own right. Think of the millions of sperm that race toward the unfertilized egg of the mother to create the zygote that started your life. Your mother chose to let you grow within her where you were nourished by the natural process of growth till you came out to this world as a living human. The process of growth continues. It may not be that easy all the time, but you are strong enough to maintain life. You are precious, and in acknowledging this fact you should value yourself and your life in all areas, praising the Creator for the wonder He has done, the wonder that is you. Nothing and no one can pull you down if you won't allow it. You are now the master of your own life, yourself particularly. You have all the choices, and you can decide what kind of life you should live. What kind of relationship you are going to compromise yourself with. Everything starts within you. Acknowledge the beauty that is you. Appreciate the life that is you. You are not a victim of circumstances if your mind refuses to accept it. Some, if not many, people wallow in the thoughts that they are victims of circumstances, such that they feel that people around them are not good to them, that they are being neglected by their parents, that they are not the favorites of their teachers in school, that their husbands cheated on them. For those who feel that their husbands cheated on them, stop feeling sorry for yourself. You are not the one cheating, so don't let the situation hurt you. You may get hurt all right, and being betrayed by a person you care so much for is a difficult and painful inner struggle, but wake up to the fact that it can only hurt you and your life if you will allow it. You are in control of your thoughts and feelings. Perhaps there is a lesson to be learned in a situation like this, so instead of feeling sorry for yourself and your life, use the situation as a lesson and an opportunity to better yourself and your life.

A long time ago when my first husband was still alive and we were together, I discovered one day that he was flirting with my sixteen-year-old housemaid. The maid told me all the details of the situation. I was terribly hurt as a result. I felt sorry for myself that I was not young anymore, and that my husband was looking for someone younger and more exciting for him to have sex with. That was a terrible feeling and a self-defeating thought process. But one day I woke up to uphold what I really was. I stopped hurting myself, my feelings particularly, and I got myself busy. I took the scholarship exam in a university, which I passed with flying colors. It boosted my self-esteem and reminded me of my strengths. I enrolled and eventually graduated with a degree.

Perhaps we invite hurtful circumstances into our lives by forgetting our self-value. If you won't allow people to run you down, you will discover that you have something special within you that is yet to be discovered and developed for your own good. So instead of allowing bad circumstances in any area of your life to constantly give you pain, discover something good within you and focus on it. What makes you happy? Discover it instead of entertaining lingering hurt feelings that won't do you any good. Tell yourself you are beautiful, you are smart, you are talented, and that life supports itself and problems resolve themselves. Just pay attention to the good things within you, even if you cannot see it or you don't believe it; bluff yourself if necessary. One day you will wake up to the truth that you are actually beautiful, smart, and talented enough to make your life beautiful and meaningful.

Do the affirmation, stand by yourself, and appreciate yourself. If you won't then who will? You are your only companion in this life twenty-four hours a day all through the years. People will come and go in your life, whether they are the ones who love and care for you or the ones who hurt you. You are the only one who stays with you and knows you inside out, so take care of yourself, love yourself like you are the most valuable thing in this life…because you are.

Your Dream Life Part 1—
Dream of an Ideal Personality

01/12/17

Do you have a dream life? What did you dream about your life when you were a teenager? Are you now living the life that you dreamed of long time ago? Does your success in having that dream come true inspire you to dream more for your future? If you are now living that life you dreamed of, how did you do it? Or if what you dreamed of never happened, do you know why? Can you make any improvements to make your dream happen? Let's go to specific areas that most people dream of in their lives; that is, if they ever dream:

1. Dream about health, beauty, looks, and total personality

2. Dream about love, relationships, and marriage

3. Dream about education

4. Dream about job or career

5. Dream about riches or money

6. Dream about material possessions, such as house and lot, cars, jewelry, home environment

7. Dream about travel and leisure

8. Dream about status quo or socioeconomic position, popularity, and reputation

9. Dream about children and family

It is said that people who don't dream will accomplish nothing in life and will just drift without direction. Many people are afraid to dream because even in the process of dreaming they only hear within themselves the opposing clatter that says "Fool, it's just a dream; it cannot happen." They kill the dream before it can even form in their heads, and many believe that the reality is doing what everybody else is doing. The truth is reality exists in the mind. Everything that exists in this world started from a mind that formed things inside it before action could be taken.

Dream of an ideal personality. What is your dream about your total personality? Can you see in your mind's eye how you would want to look? Some dreams about personality is health, physical activities such as sports, beauty, fashion, and being bright and confident in any conversational setting. It also might include having a lovable and attractive personality to easily meet new friends and become popular. Did you have dreams like these when you were a teenager? Sometimes people repeal this kind of dream because some mind clatters would block them to continue on this fantasy. Dreaming about a very attractive personality is considered vain by many, but they seem to forget that an attractive personality helps to make your dreams in everything else easy to obtain. If you have a very attractive personality, it will be easy for you to get a job and to meet your perfect mate in life, just to mention just a couple.

I remember when I was just fourteen years old, I had many fantasies about my personality, which was normal in this stage of development. I was an ugly duckling. I felt I was very ugly because most of my relatives told me so. They would compare me to my pretty cousin, Selfa. Selfa had a prettier prominent nose and a perfectly shaped face. I was considered ugly because I have very tiny nose, large eyes, very wide mouth with dark thick lips, a wide prominent-jawed face, dark skin, and curly to kinky fluffy hair. The main thing that made me feel so ugly and abnormal was when people said my legs were too long and thin, like a wild deer, plus my hips were too wide. I felt that everything about my looks was ugly from head to foot. This feeling of being ugly and discriminated against made me really sad and affected my moods daily.

One day I was looking at the pictures of the *Free Press* magazine that my dad brought home. I looked at those beautiful ladies in a world-class beauty pageant. It was actually the Miss Pacific pageant, and the winner was a Filipina beauty by the name Aurora Pijuan. I felt so sad, asking myself why I was not as beautiful as she was. I scrutinized her body and face in the picture. Her legs were wonderful, her skin was fair, and she had a very pretty face with those wonderful small eyes. I really felt sorry for myself, but that experience actually triggered me to make do with whatever I was. From then on, I started to take care of my legs. I rubbed them with papaya leaves every day because I heard that papaya leaves made the skin smooth. Then I saw in the magazine an advertisement for a wonderful skin lotion by Jergens. I bought a bottle of it and started using it on my whole body. I also asked my mom to buy me multivitamins so that my legs wouldn't be skinny anymore. I started swimming regularly in the river, went bowling, played badminton, and took lots of walking including mountain climbing to develop my leg muscles. These were just some of the things I did that I believed could improve my looks and beauty. I also bought and sewed stylish dresses, bought nice shoes, bags, and other accessories to look nice anywhere I went. In my mind was a fantasy that I was beautiful and people would notice that. I may not have been the most beautiful girl to win a beauty pageant, but I was beautiful the way I was.

Not very long afterward, when I was nineteen, I heard a lot of comments like "Jenny, what did you do? You are so beautiful. Your skin is so smooth like a doll's, and your hair is so shiny..." All these comments really made me happy and helped me boost my self-confidence. From then on, I felt empowered because I knew I could take care of my looks, and I could easily achieve anything. I noticed that people were good to me.

There was this memorable experience when I was seventeen. I was then a colporteur of the International Missionary Society of the Philippines. My main job was to sell books. As colporteurs, we would knock on doors to sell books, particularly *The Science of Natural Healing*. That noon I was knocking on the door of a local public school teacher. As our conversation progressed, she challenged me to go to the office in their school. The division superintendent was there that time because they were having a seminar; sixty teachers were in attendance. She said further that if there was one in those sixty teachers who would buy my book, she would be the number two. I was stubborn and I had great confidence in myself. I loved challenges, especially those about my personal ability, so I went straight to the school. It was noon when I knocked on the door of that office. I told the guard that I wanted to talk to the superintendent. He said that the superintendent was having lunch and suggested that I come an hour later. But the superintendent heard our talk so he stood up and had a peek at the door. When he saw me he ordered the guard to let me in.

The introduction phase was great. There was lots of flattery from him. He said I was so young and beautiful with such a bright and determined mind. To make the story short, he allowed me the first one hour of the session that afternoon to speak in front of the sixty-teacher audience. Eventually, out of the sixty teachers, fifty-eight ordered books from me. It would have been all of them, but there was a set of two married couples there, and each set ordered just one book. The first teacher I had approached ordered too. That experience really boosted my self-confidence. I attributed it to my dream of having a great personality that I had worked on and eventually made come true in material reality. I felt so rich that day! I realized how important it was to have a great personality in order to make my dreams come true.

When you see defects in your looks and inner person, start dreaming of the kind of person you believe you should be, that dream will make you behave and do something to improve your situation. Once you realize that you succeeded in this area of your life, you will develop a self-confidence that will make you accomplish things you have never dreamed of before. Opportunities will present themselves, and you will respond positively. You are now living your dream, and you can say that life is wonderful. And it all began with the acknowledgment of a need and the dream of what is ideal for you.

Good luck and God bless everyone.

Your Dream Life Part 2 —
Your Dream of an ideal Romance
and Marriage Relationship

01/13/17

In THIS ARTICLE AND THE six more articles that will follow I am discussing about an individual's dream concerning certain areas of his/her life. Dreams do come true even before we realize it. The quality of your dream determines your behavior, your decision-making processes, your attitudes about your self, your character traits that you express towards other people and your environment, your general views about life and the world as a whole and the kind of life you are living and experiencing in all the phases of your development.

In the previous article I had discussed about how an ideal personality had started as a fantasy that eventually manifested in your self as you live on.

Romantic relationship is one area in life that would often encounter lots of difficult situations in life. It is wonderful as it lasts but it would leave a bitter mark within the self and even destroy a person and life as a whole eventually when it goes wrong. Romantic love is a very strong energy that oftentimes controls a person and most often too it goes beyond reason. Many lives had been destroyed because of failed romance and/or broken marriages.

What is your dream about romance or marriage relationship? I had talked to a lot of people concerning this subject. There are lots of unhappy marriages caused by so many problems such as money, children, infidelity, promiscuity, and clash of personality; it even becomes a seat of violence to the extreme.

Many people are familiar of romantic and marital problems so I won't elaborate on problems, rather I would discuss an ideal one.

There is no perfect guidelines that would work for everyone when it comes to the subject of romantic love and perfect marriage relationship. Success in this area of life depends so much on the individuals in a relationship.

First there is the question of, "can I find a man or woman who can love me for what I am?" "who would he/she be?" How would we meet and where?" I have some friends and even relatives who would ask me to help them find a man who is similar to my husband in many ways such as kind, loving and caring, to mention just a few.

I have here some proven and effective steps in finding your perfect mate. In this method you don't have to go around for the purpose of stumbling on the right person for you. These are the following:

1. Love your self truly such that you have to affirm to your self every day and in every opportunity "I love and forgive my self completely as I am." and "I am a loving and lovable person."

2. Once this affirmation has fully convinced your inner self you will be surprised that you become that person as affirmed and many people will see those qualities in you. The next thing to do is describe in details the kind of person that you would like to have a stable relationship with for example "My perfect mate is coming to me easily and effortlessly in perfect harmony. He is handsome, tall, his age is 5 years older than me or less, he is American, he is hardworking, loving, caring,kind, honest, good provider and generous..." and so forth and so on according to your real wishes.

3. Affirm this every day until you feel that you don't want to do the affirmation anymore. Then affirm "My perfect mate is coming to me easily and effortlessly in perfect harmony."

Then wait, be patient, you will never know how it is going to happen but it will happen, just do what you are supposed to do in the inner part of you. When the time comes, he/she will come exactly as you described or better; nothing can stop it...have faith. Once he comes you will live in perfect harmony.

Your Dream Life Part 3 — Your Dream of Education

January 14, 2017

LEARNING IS A LIFETIME PROCESS. Education is a person's experience that is demonstrable in his/her behavior on a daily basis. A person's education becomes him and is useful in his daily interaction with other people in any given society. While you are still alive you won't stop learning; you learn new things every day. Nobody knows everything there is to learn in this vast universe. You may live a thousand years and study every second of that period, but you still know just a dot of what is here to know. These premises give us the reason why we should focus our study on a specific field. We should have a specialized area of education to focus on and become an expert in that field. Centeredness, focus, concentration, expertise, and mastery of a certain field is the key that opens up to your reputation as a person and as you interact in your social circles. It's not your position in a certain company that makes you the real person. In the first place, you are in that position and in that company because people in such a company are convinced of your expertise, ability, and who and what you are as a person. Positions and affiliation to a certain job and company come and go as you move and evolve in life, but you carry with you who you are, what you know, and your expertise. What you are inside out as a whole and as a person lasts throughout your life. People are drawn to you because of your reputation as being good in something and for having a desirable personality that they can partake of, imitate, or follow for their own good. You share and model your knowledge to society. Though I cannot undermine the importance of having a certain high position in a given reputable company as an index to your status quo, we have to remember that it is your education and personality that brought you there. You are the permanent entity, not the position and affiliation to a certain company you work for or with. You are the only one who is permanent in your lifetime who you can carry anywhere and any time and in any given society. Now, what is your dream education? What do you like best to do to occupy your days, hours, minutes, and every moment of your life tirelessly and enthusiastically? These should be the questions you ask yourself before you can start to dream of any pursuit of education. Do you love to dance? To sing? To look beautiful for everybody to see? To create anything beautiful as objects, pictures, or paintings? Do you love to be popular of something? Do you love to be surrounded by admiring crowds? Do you love to speak in front of faithful audience? Is your curiosity about running a successful business insatiable? Do you love numbers, language, colors, or forms? Start experimenting with yourself. Go around and look for anything that inspires your mind to imagine and start working on it passionately. It is said that every person carries along with him, since conception, at least three gifts that will help him survive, even get rich, if he discovers and enhances them in his lifetime. All you have to do is discover those things that interest you and focus on them to the tiniest details to become an expert. Once you find something that is really interesting for you, can you spend all your time scrutinizing it? If you find yourself getting busy knowing or doing something about a certain thing that caught your interest, then continue doing it to your satisfaction. That is eureka! You found your gift, your treasure.

The next thing to do is follow that interest. There are schools and knowledge available on the Internet. Pursue the knowledge, the education, specialize on it, and become a professional in your field. The average person in most societies need to go to an institutionalized educational system to learn the technology and get the title of their expertise. This is one setback for those who started to desire education. They focus more on how to go to school to get a degree, and then there are 101 problems that enter their minds to blow up the pursuit, such as lack of money, being too old, not bright enough, nobody to support them financially, people disagree with their plans, etc. All types and degrees of things block your mind. Is it the degree you want? Or is it the knowledge and the objective of improving yourself and your life? Or is it the collection of all sorts of problems to block your progress that occupy your mind? C'mon people, DREAM! That is your refuge and your ticket to life. If you won't dream, nobody will dream for you, not even your parents. They may dream for you in a certain way, but that is not *your* dream. You will have no enthusiasm to follow through thick and thin if it's not your own dream you are following.

When I talk about education, my son always pops out in my mind. My son did not finish his degree. His reason was he already had a family to support and the most important thing for him to do was to have an income. I had enrolled him in third year Computer Science, but he declined to go to school. He said he would learn the hard way, his own way to pursue a dream. He never finished his degree, but his dream came true. He is now the CEO of a million-pesos international franchise business in the biggest city of the country. His ticket? A DREAM come true that he followed passionately and enthusiastically. He would go seventy-two hours without sleep, learning the knowledge to use for his dream business. His gift? A sharp mind, and he used it to pursue knowledge on his own accord, not through formal education. But this is a rare case.

Study the life of many successful people. How did they pursue knowledge? Study Bill Gates, Ford, Thomas Edison, Lesley Brown, etc. Know how they got their expertise. School is for those who are inclined to it and can afford it, but there are many ways to pursue education that is within an individual's convenience. The key is DREAM your EDUCATION, and, for God's sake, pursue it in any way you can. Good luck and God bless everyone.

Your Dream Life Part 4 — Your Ideal Job/Career

January 15, 2017

To RECAP, THE FIRST THREE articles were about your ideal personality, your romantic/marriage relationship, and your ideal education. You have noticed by now that once you learn to love, honor, and value yourself, it would be easy to know what kind of love and partner that matches and inspires you. You are now an inspired person, the kind of inspiration that leads you to discover your inner talents and abilities that motivate you to educate yourself according to your choice. Once you have decided the kind of education you want to pursue, then it's time for you to get a job or a career. Once your dream life in these three areas are met, getting a job is so much easier. But a word about a job.

Don't get just a job for quick cash. Build a career, meaning, once you get the job you want, enhance your skills and qualifications in the job and do it well; walk the extra mile. Like everything else in this life, jobs come and go, but if you have skills and education, opportunity will present itself for you to get a job wherever you are. So what is your dream job? Can you picture it in your mind? If you want to be a doctor, can you see in your mind doing what doctors do? Wearing what doctors wear? It's the same with other professions. Do you want to be a teacher? Can you see yourself inside the classroom giving lectures to students in front of you? Go on, imagine yourself doing the job you so desire to have. My next topic is the dream of riches. Good luck and God bless.

Your Dream Life Part 5 — Dream About Riches

January 16, 2017

BEFORE I STARTED WRITING THIS article I had scanned many pages in facebook and had seen a lot of sad stories on videos about many hard-working and well-meaning Filipina domestic helpers in the Middle East who are maltreated by their employers and worst, are not paid well. In the first place why are these people working as maids and slaves in a far away place, away from their loved ones who truly love and respect them? They land in a foreign place to sacrifice emotionally, spiritually and physically, for what? Money.

Such sad situation is a good example of low self-esteem and poverty-oriented mentality and personality. Finding very lowly jobs in a far away place is motivated by the acceptance of being poor and that they cannot think and find a good-paying job to fit their ability and personality nearby. It may be true that their motive is to support their family and give them a good life but what about you, the one who sacrifice for the family.

Just like what I said in my previous article, a dream job should be a job that you enjoy doing and which you can build a career. The job you enjoy doing should be something where you have an expertise, not just for the meager income that is oftentimes not enough to support all the needs of the family. Under the article Education, you should educate yourself to develop a skill and focus on it until you become an expert. Even if you go to work in other countries the work you should do should be in line with the one you enjoy doing such as sewing, welding, teaching and so forth because if you have skills you can work anywhere and can find a decent and respectable job.

Self-respect should be the essence, money just follow. The reason why I discuss jobs here ahead of money is because it is important to have respect to attract money.

Who wants to be poor? Everybody needs money for bills, sustenance and to enjoy life better. Money is good and everybody knows the importance of money to enjoy life to the fullest...but money won't come and stay in abundance with people who have poverty-orientation. If you believe and think that money is hard to find, it won't come to you, your belief perpetuate the financial hardship that you experience.

It's good to have plenty of money all the time, better yet, it's best to be rich.

Do you want to be rich? Do you dream to be rich one day? Are you sure you desire to be rich? Average people cannot imagine themselves being rich because they cannot believe it. Lots of people would say "I don't need to be rich, if we can eat three times a day and we don't get sick; for as long as we are together and love and care for one another we are already happy about it.

These people actually have some inner wishes to be rich but somewhere within them too is a firm voice that would block such wishes for riches before they can even start to imagine for themselves a life that is rich and with plenty of money. People are scared to think of having plenty of money because they know and have accepted within them that it is bad to even dream to become rich they cannot accept the idea of being rich because they think that there is no way for them to be rich especially when they already work hard for a living and yet money is not enough.

They cannot see even in their minds that we are all living in a rich universe and there is plenty for all of us. Hard work alone is not the ticket to riches. You have to find the right job that you enjoy doing before you can start working hard. Hard work is not always well-compensated such as a hard-working house maid, her salary would just be a very low maid's salary no matter how hard-working she is. But working hard after finding the right job through your expertise, knowledge, skill and education is the kind of hard work that would pay off ample amount of money. If you want to be rich don't think first about what you are going to do to chase money, let money, plenty of them come to you in floods of abundance. Can you believe that? If you can believe that it will happen to you. Just accept the fact that you are rich and that your riches is just waiting to be delivered to you. Start in this belief, the idea would follow then suddenly you do things that lead to your riches. The key to riches is the core belief that you are rich and start living like you are already rich. Believe it or not, if you believe you are rich then you are, if you believe it's impossible for you to get rich then your belief is true.

Your Dream Life Part 6
— Dream of Travel and Leisure

01/17/17

LIFE SHOULD BE WONDERFUL. THE opposite of a serious job is leisure. Leisure is something that one does to reward himself for doing a good job. Many people buried all their efforts and time into working hard to earn a living all day long all the days of their lives. In fact, a job one should have for a living is more productive if you do it in the spirit of fun to avoid stress. The best leisure that one can have is travel. It is more fun and the learning process is more effective and enjoyable.

Seeing and experiencing the beauty of nature and mingling with other cultures in the world makes you appreciate the beauty and abundance in life. You can appreciate life better when you experience the diversity of all creatures, natural or man-made. Dreams of travels and leisure can easily be achieved if the dreams I mentioned in the first five dreams have already been met.

At this stage, you should have accomplished the process of dreaming an ideal personality, having an inspiration by a romantic and harmonious relationship, dreamed and achieved the ideal education for you, and having a job that you dreamed of. This job should fit your educational expertise. Most importantly, you should have acquired the amount of money you dreamed of. The idea here is you do the things that please you at a time that you are away from your serious everyday routine.

Your Dream Life Part 7
—The Ideal Dream Family

01/18/17

WHEN I WAS EIGHTEEN YEARS old, I dreamed of a family of my own. I imagined my husband to be fair skinned with a prominent nose and handsome so that my children would also be handsome and beautiful, more beautiful than I am because my nose is small and my skin is dark. I dreamed that I would only have two children, a boy and a girl, in that order. When it comes to my dream of having children, I imagined my children to be beautiful, healthy, and highly intelligent; everything happened and even happened in their own children. My grandchildren are healthy, intelligent, chubby babies. Included in my dream was that my husband should have a regular job and income to support me and our children. I didn't know how it was going to happen; at that time, I didn't even have a boyfriend. There was a guy who wanted to marry me when I was nineteen, but he was not the type as far as looks were concerned. He was dark skinned and just half an inch taller than me, so I ran away. Eventually, I married and my dream of having two children, a boy and a girl, happened exactly as I dreamed. I wanted the boy to be very intelligent and the girl to be pretty. I was so glad and thankful to the Lord that my dream came true about having a family and children according to my wishes.

Since life is an evolution, lots of things can happen along the way that seem to be contrary to your wishes, but then they turn out to be blessings in disguise or necessary incidents for us to evolve into perfection as intended in our personality development. At the end of the day, the dream always comes true. I dreamed of my son being married happily and earning income that could support his family. I am so glad that everything happened exactly that way, in fact better than my dream. I can understand the importance of making a dream of anything you want to happen. Dreaming about what your family should be is fun, especially when you see that all your dreams unfold toward making them coming true. When along the way you will notice that something is not right in your husband or children you will know what to do; you have to stick to your dream.

I had been pregnant after my two children were born, but surprisingly all those pregnancies were terminated without me consciously doing anything to abort them. Our psyches know if there is something that is not part of our dream; it will find a way to redirect our paths toward the fulfillment of our dream. When I found out something was very wrong with my first husband, an opportunity presented itself for me to easily leave him, but my dream about my children continued to succeed. There are lots of miracles that happen in life just so our dreams will come true.

The husband I have now is another dream come true. I described in detail what kind of person he should be, including the nationality, age, and character traits. I also included in my dream that when I marry again my children will already live independently, so that they can survive and prosper on their own, and that is exactly what happened in the perfect time. Don't be afraid to dream. Do you have a husband who treats you cruelly? Give him to God and dream of the one who is your perfect mate. Are your children not doing well in life? Create the dream and see them being successful in your mind. Let the universe do the task of changing everything according to your wishes.

Your Dream Life Part 8 — Dream of Your Ideal Status Quo

January 19, 2017

WHAT IS YOUR ULTIMATE DREAM in life? After all your basic dreams have been met, what would be the time table of the fulfillment of your ultimate dream? What is the crowning glory, the icing on your dream life?

In Maslow's hierarchy of needs, there is the so-called self-actualization stage. After all the five steps of needs have been met, the self-actualization stage is the peak in the pyramid. I discussed in my previous articles the areas of life that dreamers go through in detail. If you are a dreamer who has discovered and mastered effective and proven techniques and methods first to dream and to make a dream come true, you would have achieved some if not all of your dreams before you make the ultimate dream in your life.

Life has various stages of development. Everybody starts at conception in the womb followed with the birth. The processes in the stages of development after birth depend so much on nature and nurture. Nature here includes the genes that you inherited from your parents. Lucky are those who have parents of wholesome genes. These genes control your intelligence, emotional, and physical aspects as a person. Once you are out in this life, your achievement and success—including their timing— is influenced by your perception and depends so much on your learning processes in a given ecology and culture. The important components mold you into a total person. Since knowledge is limited to everyone, only those who have learned to connect to the spiritual or astral level of knowing, which some would call wisdom, can attract everything that they can imagine. Self-actualization is the highest form of success that any human could reach. It comes when your status quo is actualized. In this stage, you will leave behind a legacy not only to your loved ones but to many people in your society and beyond. You will become part of history for the good deeds you left behind that many people have benefited from.

For your family and blood relatives, and perhaps some special friends and associates, you may have left ample amount of money and properties as their inheritance. Even in life you have already established a reputation of being the person many can run to for some help in kind, in knowledge, in wisdom, perhaps in money, and in many more things that people need to better themselves. These are monumental deeds that a self-actualized person perform and would be remembered, even when he is gone from this life.

Have you any dreams for self-actualization? Start dreaming now if you haven't done it yet. My next topics would be about techniques to create authentic ideal dreams based on the eight basic areas of life and how to make them come true. I will provide some exercises to follow.

Techniques and Methods Part 1 — Personality Development Techniques

January 20, 2017

So far I have discussed the eight areas in life that anyone can dream of. It's wonderful to dream, and I wonder why so many people are afraid to dream. Maybe it is because within them is the core belief that dreams stay as dreams only, that they cannot happen in the material world. They believe that dreams live in wonderland, in dreamland, or in the land of fantasy. Where is dreamland anyway? This dreamland is located in the minds of the dreamers and cannot be seen in the so-called land of reality. If this is the core belief of those who are afraid to dream, my question is, look around, look at man's creations, the technology, the skyscrapers, the airplanes, the ships, all the wonders of man-made creations, and tell me how did they start? They started in the minds of the dreamers, and when the dream manifested in material reality the world became a better place to live. The world becomes the wonderland, a place of magic through technology in addition to the already beautiful creation in nature.

Once upon a time, inventors and scientists like the Wright brothers who invented, experimented, and finally created the airplane were considered foolish dreamers because people could not believe that anything could fly except birds. But the persistence of these brothers paid off, and the world got smaller in our modern days. Everything starts with an idea and a dream. It's been common knowledge that necessity is the mother of invention. Nature hates vacuums and emptiness. If there is a need there is always a supply for such need. Hence, basic to creating a dream of your own is to acknowledge your need or want or desire. Honor your desire because it is the key to your personal evolution toward happiness in life. Life should be enjoyable; otherwise, you stop living and you just exist. Ignoring your desire just because you believe there is no way you can get it only shows that you are creating alibis to stop dreaming for a better life, better yet, you are blocking your natural flow of development to the full life you are intended to become and to have. Now let's go to the basic dream of your life, the ideal personality and the steps leading to dreaming of an ideal personality for yourself. A self-evaluation of your personality physical appearance. Evaluate your physical appearance and health.

Social Interactions

List those situations where you have experienced embarrassments in communicating with people. The way you communicate with other people determines the quality of your social life. Have you found yourself making mistakes or feeling embarrassed in what you said in a given situation with a certain person? Check yourself in this situation, review in your mind what had transpired and find some better words to say for the next time you are in similar situation.

Emotional State

Observe your feelings and reactions to criticisms and comments of other people about you. Criticisms on our physical appearance more often come from our loved ones since early childhood, from parents as a joke, from siblings and relatives to provoke or spite you for any reasons. While you won't allow anyone to despise you because it hurts your feelings and affects your mood, you still should pay attention to your feelings. Don't just ignore your reactions thereby dismissing what you feel, or worse deny the feeling without really scrutinizing in the deeper sense why you feel that way.

Physical Appearance

In evaluating your physical appearance, is there anything you can see that you think are your flaws? Check yourself on these areas: skin, hair, the shape of your face, nose, eyes, lips, mouth, teeth, ears, body, legs, being too fat or thin, etc. List those you think and feel are your flaws or ugly about you. Do these in the spirit of fun. Don't spend too much time on this activity because in actuality, you already know how you look. The purpose here is just to make you aware of what and how you feel about your looks.

I remember one good friend who asked me to help her in her seemingly serious problems. After listening to her litany for a while, I asked her, "Are you beautiful?" She was shocked on my far-fetched question, but seeing that I was serious she answered, "Only when I wear makeup and dress well."

Methods to Develop Your Attractive Personality

1. Affirmation- this is a written affirmation different from the spoken ones.

Examine your flaws in the three areas of your personality: physical appearance, social interactions, emotional state. Acknowledge your assets, meaning those things you are good at. Pat yourself on the shoulder for those good things and do affirmations for those areas you think you have flaws. Write affirmations such as: "I accept myself completely as I am." "I am for myself no matter what." "I am beautiful the way I am." "I love my smile." "I have very smooth skin on my face." "I am intelligent." "I always say the right words at the right time," and so on. The idea is for you to acknowledge the beauty that is truly you. If you won't appreciate your beauty, who else will? No matter what people say, the fact that you are in this life only means that you are God's beautiful creation. Do not compare your beauty to other people's beauty; it's theirs. You too have a beauty unique to you. Everybody is beautiful in his or her own right.

2. Drawings

Draw yourself in various situations as being beautiful and having self-confidence.

3. Collage

Collect pictures of beautiful women, cut out those pictures and replace their faces with your own face from your pictures. Paste those pictures on a poster-size cardboard, and then write "this is me (your name). I am beautiful." Then hang it on your wall.

4. Spoken affirmation

Say to yourself aloud every morning in front of the mirror, "I am beautiful." "(Your name) am beautiful." "She (your name) is beautiful." Pat your shoulder whenever you have done something good as you say, "You are really smart, (your name)." Do all these methods in the spirit of fun. This is one method of making your dream of an attractive personality real to you. Good luck and God bless.

Techniques and Methods Part 2 — How to Create and Manifest Your Dream of a Perfect Romance and Marriage Relationship

January 21, 2017

WHAT WILL YOU DO IF you meet the person who suddenly makes your heartbeat soar beyond your limits? That moment when you feel he/she is the most handsome/beautiful person you ever met, then spontaneously the desire to be close to him/her for the rest of your life is born.

Emotions, as I said in my previous articles, are the transportation that carries you to the achievement of your goals or to make your dreams come true. The days following that special meeting with that special someone will be days and nights of dreaming about the "what ifs." What if he feels the same as I do toward him? You'll have more fantasies that energize you to make wonderful plans about your future and life as a whole. If you have never fallen in love before, this feeling you are feeling now will either be dismissed as foolishness if you are not sure of yourself or will be accepted as real by your subconscious if you have experienced in your past the same feelings you have now; depending on what you heard and learned about relationships are taking charge of your thoughts and emotions. Your core belief is a series of influences from the people you grow up with and mingle with throughout life. When the time comes that your mind and heart are ready for a romantic relationship, all you have to do is dream of that someone. Describe in detail in your dream his looks, his personal traits, his emotions for you, and your emotion toward him. Don't just imagine it, feel it. This is how you are going to attract your perfect mate, let him (or her) live in your heart and mind, even if you have not met him yet in person. The perfect time will come and the opportunity will present itself. The method is simple; do this in the spirit of fun.

Drawings and Pictures

Draw a man and a woman in a romantic setting that appeals to you. Imagine or pretend that the woman is you. If you are a man and the woman is your prospective mate, do the inverse. Color your drawings with bright colors, the surroundings, your clothes, and everything else in the drawing. If you are not very good at drawing, you can make use of pictures. Cut out any picture of a man and a woman in a romantic setting, write your name on the person you signify as you and your partner, write "my perfect mate," and then write "Here I am with my wonderful perfect mate, happily spending a loving moment together. My perfect mate loves me and I love him just as much." Cut the picture out and make a poster of it. Post it on the wall of your bedroom. Do the same to the drawing if you can draw.

Next, draw you and your perfect mate on your wedding day, or cut a picture of a bride and a groom on their wedding day, replace the face of the person that you identify as you and write "This is our wedding day. My perfect mate and I are now married and are living happily ever after." The idea is have an open mind, a mind that can dream anything you want. Silence your mind from opposing clatters, and just continue to dream on what you really want to happen. You will never know how it is going to be, but the result will be according to your desire.

When my British fiancée, Colin, died of cancer, he was fifty-five and I was fifty-three. I grieved for two years and never wanted to live anymore because I thought that there would never be any man like him anymore who I could love. But then I realized that something within me was saying that I must have someone to love me because my two children each have their own family and I felt neglected. I know myself and I know what I want. I am a loving person and I must have the object of my love who can reciprocate with equal emotions and care.

One day as I was sorting out my things, I saw a poster-size picture of me standing beside the picture of Richard Gere. That picture of me was actually a picture of a model that I cut out from a magazine whose face I replaced with my own. Then I saw a big red posterboard where I pasted the picture and wrote "Me and my perfect mate." I wrote the name "Gere." I did not really mean the actor Richard Gere, but as I wrote that I was thinking about any name close to that or maybe similar. After a month of that poster on my bedroom wall, I met a man I really liked on the Internet; his name was Greg. Years later, I noticed that instead of two e's, as in Gere, there are two g's in Greg. See what I mean? Do something about your dream and fantasies. Use pictures to simulate your dream. It will work in any area of your life, even in romance. Greg and I have now been married for five years, and we are perfectly happy. And I know it will be as long as we live.

Techniques and Methods Part 3 — How to Dream and Manifest the Type of Education You Desire

January 22, 2017

WHEN A CHILD IS BORN nobody knows what she/he will become in his/her adult life. Education-wise, he/she is like an empty vessel that needs to be filled in order to survive and, most importantly, eventually become useful to any unit of society where he/she belongs. From then on, the baby learns something by the moment. He learns how it feels when he needs food and how to let anyone around know of his need or feeling for the moment. The process of learning continues and develops. The speed and nature or type of education is dependent on how a particular need is met as it arises in any given time and the individual's perception and reaction to any given response.

In the early stages of development from birth through puberty, and even up to late teenage years, education is not much of a person's choice but is imposed on him by institutionalized and standard education and the culture of a given social structure. Even so, a person already shows some inclinations at an early age regarding what he likes to do. Although, these are also influenced by the people around him and the total environment. Human beings are privileged to have the gift of a thinking mind. This mind can either make or break his life depending on its interest and contents. Among the many functions of the mind is to think, analyze, observe, plan, create, and dream or fantasize. A beautiful mind is one that has learned to discipline and establish methods in order to thrive and succeed in facing various complexities in living. Many times in some close-knit family ties and some cultures, parents dream for their children and plan for their future including what education they should attain. There is a big problem in this situation, even if the parents are well-off and can afford to send their children to school. In the end, it is still the person himself who will make decisions for himself and his own life. This is the reason why it is important for a person to dream of what kind of education he wants to pursue, what kind of skills he wants to develop, and so forth.

When my son was sixteen years old, I wanted him to continue his study in college and to finish a medical degree. I wanted him to be a doctor. His father on the other hand wanted him to be an engineer or a lawyer. He had been an A student ever since he entered school for the first time. We were a proud parents, and everybody knew that our son was very intelligent and popular being so. But to my dismay, my son wanted nothing of our suggestions. He just wanted to be a musician, a guitar player in particular. He ran away from home, and at seventeen he became a father to a daughter. Then on his eighteenth birthday, he married the mother of his daughter. Since then, his life became miserable. He was a young, jobless father and husband. He suffered not only having nothing to feed his young family but was despised by everybody, especially his wife and the relatives of his wife. Since I am the mother, an educator, I could not allow those things to happen to my son, so I started to open his mind to the reality of living. My son learned his lesson and he redirected his life. Now, he is the CEO of his own international franchise with Vanguard International.

Life is a complex of challenges, dreams, and failures. When you are young you are vulnerable to make mistakes, but it's all right if you learn from your mistakes. Having an education from schools and universities is a standard method to pursue an education that could easily get you standard jobs and standard income. It's a good and easy way to success if you you can afford it. If you think you are poor and cannot afford formal education, then just dream of that which you want to become. For example, if you want to be a doctor at the age of thirty and you are still fifteen, if your desire to become a doctor is very strong, then pursue it in your dream. Don't worry yet about money; otherwise, you will have no chance to achieve your dream because what you worry about is what will come true, not the dream. What you can do here is first, make use of the visual suggestion. Draw yourself as a doctor or cut pictures of a doctor at work. As usual, replace the face of the doctor with your own and then write "Here I am, a doctor curing my patient." Post it on the wall of your room. This method is called visual suggestion. Let that vision of you being the person you want to become stick in your mind through visual suggestion. And since you are interested in becoming a doctor, follow where your interest leads you. Follow the dictates of your mind; you will be guided by your instinct. The point is learn to follow what you really want, and focus on it. Do not follow the worries and the problems that can block what you really want to be, to do, and to have in the future.

An Ad Lib for Today—Esperanza

January 23, 2017

LIKE I MENTIONED IN MY other articles, life is full of twists and turns. We can create beautiful dreams and pursue them in effortless manners if we know how. But along the way there are challenges that we meet, and we are obliged to face them for the moment before we can proceed.

I woke up early this morning only to receive the sad news of my biological mother's death; she died just an hour before I woke up. Earlier in December last year, I was elated to learn that my biological mother was still alive. We had one video cam talk via Skype. I had expressed to her my reasons for being so nasty to her when I met her in person when I was twenty-five. I told her that the next time we met would be different because I had mellowed and had forgiven her. At the time we first met, my bad experience was still fresh in my mind. I could still remember when I was four and my sister was two years old when we were left at the house of my aunt Tutay who was a Spanish teacher and was out every day to work. There was a maid by the name Josefa who would beat us with a broom when we were left alone with her. I was very sad and angry at why we were left there by our mother and father. My anger stayed with me. Since that time, I met my biological mother again when I was already a mother myself at twenty-five. I already had two children. I remember telling my biological mother, Esperanza, that she was the most unforgivable woman to me. I said further that the most unforgivable woman in the world is the mother who would leave her small children. Esperanza was a wonderful and loving woman and she tried to explain the situation, but I wouldn't listen at the time. For me, nobody could understand my miserable experience with that maid, and all because our mother left us. That was all I could think of. Now I feel so sad that I have no more chance to meet her again to express to her that I have forgiven her, that I have no more anger left in my being, that I can understand now that all things work together for good.

This morning I was surprised that I woke up so early, it was four in the morning when I suddenly got up and went straight to my computer. It was a feeling that there was something in my computer, some message perhaps that there would be some change in what I would do today, something different from what I planned to do. True enough, as I opened my Facebook page, I received a message from my niece in the Philippines telling me that my biological mother had died. So this is the change. I am going to write about my mother and why her death was such a sad incident for me. It's not just the sadness of losing a mother; it's a sadness of not having the privilege to know her well enough.

I grew up with my dad and his wife who I had known to be my mother. When I was delivering my firstborn, a woman told me that I had a mother who delivered me to this world just like what I just did at that time. I was confused at first, until she told me that the name of my biological mother was Esperanza. Here is an excerpt of what I wrote years back about Esperanza. I entitled it: "Mama, Who Is Esperanza?"

"Genevieve." I heard again, that remotely familiar small voice calling that equally familiar name that I sometimes heard inside my head, especially when my eyes were heavy as I was gradually drifting to sleep. My heart skipped a beat; the voice seemed real though in a whisper. I never turned my head, as I was so focused on what I was doing.

I was some meters away from the group comprising my eleven-year-old elder stepsister Julia, the three-year-old little sister Lily, and my one-year-old youngest brother Junior.

Julia was babysitting the little ones; they were playing on that sandy bank of the river under the shade of the huge bridge over the Cagayan De Oro City River. She buried the little bodies of my siblings with sand but with their faces out; they looked very relaxed.

Whereas, I was the independent one and I kept myself away from them because I was looking around for stickier sand to form into sand balls. I had created several of them, and I exposed them under the heat of the sun hoping that once they were dry they wouldn't break.

Papa and Mama were busy doing the laundry at the river. It was a Sunday and this was one of those Sundays where the whole family had a picnic at the beach or in the river to wash the accumulated sheets and blankets and other laundry.

"Genevieve..." I heard the voice again, and this time it was very close to my ears; it was a deep, airy whisper. I was scared but I turned my head up at my side to see a smartly dressed lady squatting beside me and looking down at me. I was sitting with my legs spread wide and relaxed on the sand. She was about to hug me, but she seemed to observe my facial expression and reaction on seeing her, hoping perhaps that I still recognized her.

She was so beautiful and very tall, and her hair was shoulder length and beautifully wavy. Her eyes were wide with thick lashes, but I saw the tears in her eyes. I was a bit nervous and suspicious, remembering the mora(a mora was known to be a long-haired Muslim woman who tie her hair up into a coil, she kidnaps children to be fed to the mine and we children thought that a mine is a huge monster that looks like a gigantic alligator), but no, she did not look like a mora. I just stared at her very long while teardrops fell on her cheeks. Then she asked, "Genevieve, do you remember me?"

I just blinked, confused why she was calling me Genevieve; my family called me Deden and that was the name I knew for myself. She seemed familiar but I just couldn't remember who she was, so I asked, "What is your name?" in which she answered, "Esperanza, remember me?" She forced herself to smile as she reiterated.

No, I didn't remember. It must have been two years ago since we were separated; I learned very much later that I was barely three and a half years old when Papa took me and my siblings away from her. I was five years old this time.

Julia saw me and Esperanza talking so she called me and told me to run away to Mama and Papa, as she herself ran down to the river where Papa and Mama were washing the laundry. She was panicky as she screamed to them. I was confused of Julia's behavior and it scared me; I did not understand any word in her screams.

I became panicky too, so I stood up quickly and attempted to run away, but Esperanza grabbed me and hugged me tight. She stood up and carried me as she ran to cross the road. I was kicking and screaming and tried hard to let go of her, but I could hear her very sad and loud cry as she screamed "Genevieve, I am your mother!"

Everything happened so quickly, and I found myself pulled away in opposite directions. Papa and Mama were pulling me away from Esperanza while Esperanza wouldn't release her hold of me. They were playing tug-of-war with me; I was the rope.

Esperanza was no match in this tug-of-war. I was the one hurt badly. I still had the trauma when I woke up in the hospital the next morning.

This incident never left my mind, and even to this day I find it so difficult to trust the people who are supposed to love me.

One day, years later, when I asked Mama who was Esperanza, she just answered, "She was your nanny when you were a baby."

Techniques and Methods Part 4 — Techniques and Methods to Dream and Manifest Your Ideal Job

01/24/17

IF YOU ALREADY HAVE A dream job in mind, what you should do next is to do some techniques and methods to make it happen effortlessly. But you have to remember that you have to first have the education needed to have that job you really want to do. If you don't know yet the right job for you, you have to ask yourself: Do I really want to work? Do I work for money? For prestige? Or just to have something to do? Many, if not most, people work to live, to pay pressing bills, and to keep life going. If you work for these objectives, the tendency will be that you will eventually diminish your energy because you are chasing all the pressing situations that involve money. When this happens, you have to slow down and consult your inner self. Ask yourself: Is this how I want to live my life? Is this the job that I really enjoy doing? The answers will come to you. It may be that you don't really like your job for many reasons, but you are just obliged to work because of necessities. When you find the answers, start changing the situation in your mind. Start seeing yourself in your mind doing what you love to do. You may not leave your present job immediately, but you have to do something so that you will get the kind of job that you really love. Once you have discovered what you really want to do, here are some suggestions:

- Look on the Internet and find the kind of job people do that you also want to do. Find pictures of them and then print them out.

- Find some magazines where your favorite job is published. Then cut them out and replace the face of the person who does the job that you like doing with your face. Make a poster out of this picture, post it on your wall, and write: "Here I am doing the job that I really like to do."

- Determine how much you desire to earn from that job. On the picture write: "Here I am doing the perfect job for me from which I am earning (say the amount). Posting something like that on your wall while you continue with your present job will remind your psyche what you really want to do, and sooner or later the opportunity or an idea will come to you. Just believe in yourself.

- Another method is visualization and affirmation, but this method is already visualization that would eventually convince your psyche. What is most important is the subconscious mind must be convinced, and then everything will be easy. The bottom line here is to familiarize yourself in the inner part of your being through imagination the kind and the details of the job you so desire to have; by doing this your subconscious mind will begin to accept the situation as true which then cause the opportunities to present itself to you and not only that, you will also recognize such opportunities and you begin to act according to your capacity.

Techniques and Methods Part 5 — Visualizing, Drawing, Collage, and Simulation

01/25/17

YOU SHOULD HAVE NOTICED BY now that the common techniques and methods to dream and manifest that I discussed in my previous articles had something to do with imagination, affirmation, visualizing, drawing, collage, and simulation. The objective in these methods is to convince your subconscious mind what you want. These methods, when done regularly, will finally enter your brain's right hemisphere and that is all you need. Once they enter into your psyche, things will start to change in your life in that particular area.

How to Manifest Money

Using the same method, draw bundles and bundles of money with you counting them, or you may cut out pictures of bundles of money or print out from those you find on the Internet, and then make a poster out of it with your picture in the center of the poster counting the money. At first, you may feel like you are crazy, but just continue doing it, knowing that the effort must be done to convince yourself. So whether you believe it or not—or you feel like you are crazy—just do it. Do you want to be rich? Then do it. Say the affirmation aloud to yourself every day: "Money, come to me easily and effortlessly in very satisfactory and harmonious ways for the highest good of all concerned." Also write every day for twenty days: "I, (your name, example, Jenny), am rich, well, and happy. She is rich, well, and happy. Jenny is rich, well, and happy." You have to write these affirmations twenty times for twenty days using these three persons. Don't ask questions. Do you want to be rich? Just do it and see what happens. In all my techniques and methods to manifest, I take advantage of pictures, words, and simulation. It's not important if you believe or not; if you keep doing it something within you will get the point and lots of good things will happen in your life. Sometimes we call it good luck, but in truth, it's the energy within you that attracts the universal energy that jibes with your own. There are many methods that also make use of audio-visual activities. The more senses you use to attract those things you desire, the more effective they will get. Later on you will find ways on your own as you continue, and you will discover what is effective for you.

What I have discussed here has worked for me many times, and they are so miraculous. I used them in all areas of my life, and they all manifested in perfect timing. Whether its money, job, love life, family, travel and leisure, education, social interaction, or everything else that matters to me, these methods work. Just have patience and perseverance. It's not necessary that you believe it; the truth is there regardless of your reaction to it. A person born blind has never seen any color in his life, but he cannot say that there is no such thing as red because he cannot see it. Whether he sees or not, and whether he believes of its existence or not, all colors exist. We are all like that. Most human beings are blind to the truth of the existence of many important universal laws or the works of the spirit, so many don't believe. But just like the blind person, whether human beings believe or not is not important; the universal laws and the spirit world exist. Hence, just do the methods that can connect to the universal laws, regardless of your belief.

Faith that Makes Life Beautiful

January 26, 2017

Do you have difficulty believing in your dream? Do you worry that you have done all the techniques and methods yet nothing happens? If this is the case, then develop faith. Faith is a gift, a reward to those who put effort for their desire to let faith work in their lives. The Bible says in Luke 17:6 KJV that "if you have faith as small as a mustard seed, everything will be possible for you; you can move mountains." See? Faith is magic. If you just have faith, then there is no place for doubts and worries in your life.

I used to be a skeptic because of my experience when I was a child. My dad was a preacher and I looked up to him, but he had failed to fulfill promises he made to me, which, to me, were very important. I was so disappointed and devastated that it affected my relationships. It broke me and broke my life eventually. That remorse stayed with me until I found a way to develop faith. Faith is an extremely powerful virtue that never fails. There was a time in my life when I felt, *I just have to give up belief in everything.* I wished I would stop believing in God or in anything that could not be proven by science and the logical studies. I was so angry and I constantly got into trouble with anyone I encountered; I was very disrespectful and rude. Because of my anger, my bad behavior with everyone gradually affected my life. All my friends were gone, even my relatives were scared of me. I was very independent so I thought, *I don't need them anyway.* I didn't care if I had no friends. But then the problem multiplied.

Even my son had a troubled life. He married at eighteen and became a father that year. He was jobless and had quit school, and there was no way that he could support his young family. My son's difficulty was a wake-up call for me, so I decided to go back to God and asked for guidance. It did not take long before I found a book in National Book Store in Manila entitled *Creative Visualization* by Shakti Gawain. Such a book was an extreme blessing to me. I followed all the instructions there diligently. I was not even sure if I believed all it. There was a segment in that book that discussed just in passing on how faith could be developed; just a little mention and it opened my mind. The reason I discuss faith here is because I have proven to myself what faith can do in our lives. I would like to share here one of the many miracles that happened to me and my family because of faith. Faith is a sense of knowing that something you desire is coming true or is happening.

The birth of my twin grandchildren

Leizl, the first wife of my son, was worried on the fifth night after she delivered the twins. It was such a critical situation; she almost lost her life during that delivery. The twins formed a T inside her womb, and there is no way they could come out normally, so a caesarian section operation was necessary. But my son, only twenty-three years old at the time, had no money for the operation. He only had P2,000 ($40) in cash, not even enough for a normal delivery, so he decided to wait awhile instead of immediately following the doctor's order to go to the hospital that Friday evening. He was still going to see if he could take out a loan from his employer. That Friday evening, Leizl had a hemorrhage so we quickly took her to the hospital on emergency. She lost a lot of blood and a blood transfer of three bags was necessary to save her life. Each bag cost P2,500. ($50)It was a life-and-death situation, and the hospital wouldn't dispose the blood on credit. Then the employer of my son paid for the blood.

On the fifth day, Leizl was well enough to go home and was worried about the bill. It was hospital policy to not let patients leave the hospital until all the bills were paid. That night while Leizl was sleeping, I went into deep meditation and then I opened my eyes to stare at the brightly lit ceiling. As I was doing that, I willed to see the image of Leizl and the babies already lying on their bed at home, and amazingly I saw the image very clearly.

The next morning was a Saturday, and Sunday would be a holiday, which meant that if we could not go home that day, the bill would increase and the more difficult it would be for us to go home. Leizl told a nurse to get our bill while I was talking to one of the four doctors who delivered Leizl's twins. Before the doctor came into our room, Leizl was telling me her worries. She said that if the bill reached P20,000,($400) then there was no way we could go home today. I told her, "We can go home, just have faith and stop worrying." But she continued to worry all the same. While I was talking to the doctor, the bill was brought in and it caused Leizl to turn pale; the bill was P43,000($800). When the doctor left, she was already crying as she pointed at the bill. I saw it but I told her, "We can go home today. I don't care how much the bill is." My son at that time was still working in his office. It was already 3:00 in the afternoon, and the cashier's office would close at 6:00 p.m. Leizl was very fidgety, murmuring to herself that it was impossible to find that amount of money in just three hours. I told her that God was richer than anyone in the universe. Leizl didn't believe it or maybe was fed up with my declarations of faith in situations like this. She probably thought, *What we need now is money, not some sermon on faith.*

Meanwhile my son stood up and walked toward his own rented office at the nearby three-story building whose owner was a millionaire. As he was climbing up the stairway, he met the janitor who acknowledged him saying, "The boss has been asking about you. He heard that your wife delivered the twins and he was wondering why you did not pay him a visit to announce the news." For this, my son went to see the boss (Prescripto), and in the midst of their conversation he said to my son, "Get the bill, and let me have the privilege to pay for it." Prescripto was superstitious. He believed that boy-girl twins was lucky for his business. So, all the bills were paid completely by Prescripto, and true to what I saw on the ceiling the night before, the mother and the twins were lying on their own bed at their home that day, exactly as I saw it.

Faith is seeing what others cannot see. When your faith is strong, you can see what is not happening yet.

If there is any skill you should want to develop in your life, let it be FAITH, the kind of faith that makes things happen to you according to your clear intention and wishes. Let faith do the magic.

You Are as Rich as You Can Imagine

January 27, 2017

SUCCESS STARTS FROM THE RICH imagination of the mind. The heart desires fulfillment the moment it senses the need or lack of something in a given situation. The mind responds to the senses, and then it conceptualizes the ways and means to meet such needs from which the mind bases its decision for action that the body executes.

Abundance and riches are dependent on how the mind defines success and the feeling of satisfaction from the heart. But since man's desires are insatiable, the mind continues to conceptualize on ways and means to meet the desires of the heart, and the cycle continues in a spiral and evolving manner. The greatness of success, abundance, and riches are dependent on the intensity of the heart's desires, the strength of the determination of the mind's willpower, and the body's responses to these two forces, plus the skills in the coordination of these three basic components of the creature called man. A man, therefore, is as rich as he can imagine. Hence, anyone who wants to get rich should start studying his own mind. How one lives his life is the result of how one uses his mind.

My Love Charm Collage

January 28, 2017

ARE YOU LONELY AND NEEDING somebody who could be your perfect mate? Be creative. Make a collage just as I did long time ago before my hubby and I met and eventually married. Here's the story of my collage.

The Collage That Materialized My Wish for a Perfect Mate

Every now and then everybody wishes for something to have and to happen in his life; these wishes could be objects, people, relationships, or important incidents that seem impossible in a certain time. When these wishes become dominating thoughts that develop into desire, the mind takes over; it starts to surmise on the wistful thinking and the question: what if I could...? which triggers the mind to see some possibilities through imagination and observation. Then the mind plans, based on its observations and perceptions. My mind did just that.

In September 2010 while I was living alone in my apartment and teaching at the same time, I suddenly felt lonely, which made me say to myself, "I wish I had a new husband to loves me and cares for me and vice versa..." This was also in the second death anniversary of my fiance. It was just a wish, but as the days went by, that wish nagged at me like its urging me to do something about it and seemingly having a life of its own. Then one day while I was sorting out the projects of my students in my bedroom, I noticed the bright red, wide poster board; it looked so attractive like it was urging me to do something about it and display it somewhere. So I picked it up and stared at it like something within me was asking what I could do to it. I sat down, took a pair of scissors, and started cutting it into a big heart shape. Without much thinking, I took my big picture from my file and pasted it in the center of the heart. While observing it, I noticed that something was missing so I sorted through my files of pictures and magazines until I saw the picture of Richard Gere that matched the size of my picture. I cut it and pasted it beside my picture and under his picture I labeled it "Richard Gere". Under my picture is the label Jenny. I decorated the poster board some more and posted it on the wall inside my bedroom. It was right beside my dressing table so that I noticed it every morning when I got ready for work. I liked the poster and it made me smile and murmur some crazy loving words to myself every time I happened to glance at it. When the clock struck midnight on February 14, 2011, Greg had just arrived at the airport at NAIA, Manila, Philippines, and we had our first hugs. In retrospect, I noticed that the red heart symbolizes Valentine's Day for me. I also notice some other coincidences such as the fiance that I was really waiting to come in April of 2011 was named Rick but Greg, who was not my fiance, came on the day of the heart. Greg is double "g" and Gere is double "e." Are these merely coincidences or is my psyche responsible for this? I am now creating collages that can trigger coincidences for the things I wish for. Such coincidence!

Three Reliable Inner Strengths to Summon at Life's Lowest Times

January 29, 2017

LIFE IS WONDERFUL WHEN EVERYTHING works well and you are at its peak of success. But then life's journey is full of ups and downs and twists and turns. When we are on the right path of our journey, we travel safely and swiftly, but many times we get lost and that can lead to danger, which can then lead us to a dead end. Do you wonder why many people commit suicide? Imagine this situation. You are lost in a wild jungle with ferocious beasts and you cannot find your way out. Suddenly, right at your back is a lion ready to attack you. The natural instinct is to gather all your energy and run as fast as you can away from the chasing lion. You try to run to the left but a pack of hungry wolves sees you and are preparing to attack you. You try turning to the right, but an angry and hungry tiger is running toward you. You lift your head up hoping for a rescue, but instead there's a hovering vulture waiting for your dead body. So you run fast forward because you see a cliff. You had thought of just jumping down to save your dear life, but then you see a group of huge, hungry crocodiles opening their mouths expecting your fall. That's a dead end. That's your life's ending. Dead. This story is an allegory of what I experienced some time in the past. That was exactly how I felt in my situation that I labeled my "dark ages." Why?

First, my son dropped out of school at seventeen and was now a jobless father of three little children ages five and the twins less than a year. Second, I was completely broke and was jobless too. My husband had just died, leaving us nothing but hundreds of thousands of dollars in debt. With my daughter in college, I didn't even have money or the source of income to support our survival needs. Third, we were to be evicted from our home because it had been three months that we were unable to pay the rent. Fourth, our electricity had been cut, and we were literally living in the dark. I had three hungry babies, my family was broke, and nobody was earning money. How was I to survive? Good question. I did some introspection and meditation until I discovered the answers to our dilemma.

I believed in the principle of "this too will pass," that it was just one wrong turn in life's journey, a mistake. And since it was a mistake, it could be corrected and we could learn some valuable lessons from it. There was no easy way to get out from that situation. It was high time for me to look inside. I just had to stop running and trying to evade and escape. The normal behavior in this situation would have been to go around begging for help from everyone, from friends and relatives. But then my value system wouldn't allow me to live the life of a mendicant. I knew there was a fountain of strength within me, enough to defeat any attacks on my life from any direction. The key word is: remember. Remember who you are. Remember love. Remember faith.

Using this principle, I wrote in narrative form every major positive past event of my life where I felt like I was a superstar. I remembered my achievements in school where I graduated from elementary as valedictorian, my being the eldest child and being pampered by my parents and whole family, my happy childhood, my friends and colleagues who believed in me, and my promotions and commendations at work. I kept myself busy "metaphorming" or simulating, drawing, sketching, coloring, and writing down beautiful memories of my hey days, writing affirmations. I remembered in detail, repeating and hearing in my mind the appreciations and admiration of the people around me when they believed in me. Then I thanked my God for creating me the way I am. There are always good things about us and good memories to remember. Remember love. I remember being loved by my parents and family; I remembered how I loved them. I remember everything I value and love, such as pets, work, hobbies, small possessions, God, nature, and any beautiful things that attract me. Remember faith. I remembered that faith was a magic word. I closed my eyes and meditated, seeing in my mind's eyes the beauty of life, my beautiful grandchildren wearing beautiful clothes, eating nutritious food, and being very healthy. I saw in my mind's eyes the transformation of my life and my family's life when the situation would change. I kept telling myself, "These too will pass. Problems resolve themselves. Life supports itself." The situation may not have changed abruptly, but it's this process of "remembering" that brought us through during the difficult times.

I remember one day, when my twin grandchildren were two years old, their mother went out to clean houses for cash to buy food for the children for that day. The twins told me that they were hungry, so I asked them what they would like to eat. Moj, the little girl twin, said that she would like to eat spaghetti. Pokoy, the boy twin, said that he would like to eat fried chicken. I told them to help me find a picture of those foods from the magazines I had shown them. When they had indicated what they wanted, I cut them out and pasted them on a posterboard. I decorated it and posted it on the wall of my bedroom. I told them to make a sound together like they were chanting. I had read somewhere in one of my books that the chant that says, "Om mani padme aum." I let them memorize that and that was what we three were chanting as we faced the poster of the food on the wall. It did not take very long before I heard a call from outside; it was the janitor in the Pro-Gloria Headquarters. This was a political headquarters during election campaign season. The office was just across the street from our apartment. The janitor was outside the door, and he was carrying many small Styrofoam boxes of food. He said that the man in charge of the office sent him to deliver the food because McDonalds gave him too much food. He could not eat it all and he thought the children might like it. McDonalds was the sponsor of the party and supplied them with food every day. There were a dozen boxes of spaghetti,(the spahetti came from Jollibee, the Filipino owned competitor of McDonald, fried chicken, and rice) McDonald in the Philippines also serve rice as it is the staple food of the country. We were excited! But it was just the beginning. Every day there was an excess of food supply in that office so they gave us food every day. Aside from that, I was hired to work in that office as the one in charge of the distribution of all the election paraphernalia. Being head of the office I was able to hire temporary employees to distribute the parapernalia to the public, so I hired my daughter-in-law and my daughter. We all had jobs this time and the children never went hungry again. I know how faith works, and I know in my heart completely that problems resolve themselves. Both good and difficult times pass; nothing is permanent.

How to Develop Strong Willpower
the Useless Way

January 30, 2017

WHAT IS WILLPOWER AND WHY is it important to a dreamer? If faith is magic that makes everything possible and brings to you whatever you desire, then willpower is faith's tool, its machine gun, its implementer, its delivery car that carries and delivers to you the good that you deserve or that belongs only to you. I had this experience concerning willpower.

I was in the delivery room of the Maternity Hospital when I delivered my daughter on November 11, 1979. After the baby came out, the doctor gave me general anesthsia and then sewed stitches on my sex organ to make it smaller. I was allergic to anesthesia. Its effect on me would either be that I could still feel the pain or if overdosed I would die. The hospital had no sophisticated diagnostic tools to ensure that their medicines worked for particular patients like me. His first injection was not effective, so I screamed that the anesthesia did not perform correctly. I could still feel the horrible pain, so he increased the dose, which only proved fatal because it started to kill me, literally. I almost died of an overdose. My breathing stopped and the doctor and his assistant did everything to bring me back. While in this situation I felt like I was suddenly falling down to a bottomless dark pit. I saw myself covered with a pink jelly-like surrounding; it was like a room but there was no space. I was wondering why I could still breathe when there was no space for air in that room. Everything around was solid pink, and then I saw psychedelic lights. All colors were moving in chaotic forms. I asked myself if I was still alive and in the world of the living. I also asked if I could get out of this situation. I saw no door, no outlet; it was like I was inside a solid rock but it was soft, perhaps a solid pink jelly. After asking how I could get out of there, a sense was saying something to me. I knew it was there just watching me, but the message did not come as words. It was just a sense or an inner feeling. It said, "Will it and everything you want comes true." As soon as I sensed the message, I willed it. I told myself, "I am getting out right now," and instantly my eyes opened and I started to breathe normally. The doctor and his assistant were elated that I was back to life. From that time onward, I used the principle of willing what you want in life. I have faith in affirmations because it is how we will what we want in life.

If we say to ourselves, "I am rich, well, and happy," poverty, lack, and illness will keep away from us. Now, seeing the importance of willpower, you may say, "I willed a lot of things but nothing happened to me according to my wishes." The answer may be that your willpower is not strong enough. Most people try to dream and will what they want but of no effect. It's because when they will, another mind clatter grabs the will, instead of trusting that what you will is happening already. What comes in is the statement of doubt: "I wish it will come true," and then another follow-up clatter says "Foolishness! Stop fantasizing. Work hard instead!" And another and another. Millions of blocks will attack your already weak will. Remember that doubt is the opposite and enemy of faith. If you doubt, your will will do the opposite of what you wish for. Whimsical wishing is the opposite of strong willpower. A wish is just a wish. A wish means that what you want is impossible to happen, so it is. Are you ready to develop your strong willpower? Here are funny ones.

Remember, do this in the spirit of fun: "Useless Exercises" for Strong Willpower.

Strong willpower is a result of consistent exercise and self-discipline. Purposeful physical exercises such as to lose weight are illustrative of purposeful mental or willpower exercises to develop a strong willpower; in fact, willpower exercises include physical and behavioral demonstrations. In the following suggestions of willpower exercises, the only rule is "don't question the exercises; just do it." Otherwise, you will go back to your habitual rationalization and the exercises will lose their value. Here are five effective "useless exercises" to develop a strong willpower (you can do all of them or choose just one): I use the term "useless exercises" as an idiomatic expression indicating the seemingly nonsense and illogical activities but they are actually effective for this particular objective, for the will;

1. Find a place where nobody and nothing can see or distract you. Set a consistent time every day. Do this "useless" exercise ten minutes a day for thirty days. Stand on a chair without stepping down for ten minutes.

2. Write the following statement a hundred times every day for thirty days. "I will write a useless exercise."

3. For five minutes a day, for thirty days and in a place where you cannot be distracted, repeat the following to yourself, aloud or quietly while racing the clock: "I will do this."

4. Also in a place where nobody and nothing can distract you, do the following for ten minutes: Walk back and forth from wall to wall in a room.

5. For five minutes a day and for thirty days, same time every day, do the following: Step up and down on a chair. Forward step up, step back down.

There you go. Just do them in the spirit of fun. I did them and I got the reputation of being straightforward and with unbending determination. Remember, don't question it. Good luck, guys!

Solving Problems the "Outside the Box" Way

January 31, 2017

THEY SAY THAT PROBLEMS ARE part of life. Problems come in various forms and in many areas of life. Most problems are the results of wrong decisions and mistakes in handling situations. To mention a few perennial common problems in life: financial problems, inability to pay bills, indebtedness, relationships or marriage, cheating spouses, jealousy, control, domestic violence, juvenile problems of children, addictions, education, failed dreams and plans, job-related problems or joblessness, health or medical issues. Problems can become complicated and serious depending on the problem-solving ability of the person in question. There are minor problems that are encountered on a daily basis, and there are major perennial problems that stay for a lifetime. These problems are destructive to life if left unchecked and unsolved because they will multiply. They invite more and more clans related to the original problems in a very long-term basis. Many people try to solve their problems by creating more problems to themselves; for example a teen age girl who cannot bear anymore to stay with her parents because she is always scolded so she thinks that the solution of her problem is to elope with her boy friend only to find out in the long run that it was a big mistake when she discovered that her boy friend was violent in their relationship. I would like to cite one experience here of a problem I had when my second husband died.

His corpse had been in the funeral parlor for three weeks. I could not bury his corpse for two serious reasons: one, I had no money to pay for a burial ground in the cemetery, and two, the bill for the funeral parlor was P140,000 ($2, 080), but I was completely broke, not even a penny to my name. I could not pay the bill, so the funeral parlor wouldn't release the body until I cleared all the bills. The longer the body stayed there the bigger the bill became. It's true I had received some donations at the vigil from friends who had visited the funeral, but the money gathered was not even enough to feed the visitors who'd come for some services. My best friend Engineer Veronica Malano Miguel saw the grave problem that I had so she offered to lend me P80,000, that's one half the amount of the fee. She said she had to sell her car. I thanked my best friend for her generous plan to help me, but I told her, "Your desire to help me will cause you problems. You will lose the car that you need, and I cannot see any way that I can pay you back in the near future." Then I told her that I would just solve my problem on my own term without creating any more problems. The best way to solve problems is to let problems solve themselves with the premise that "life supports itself." People solve the problems in the way they know based on their experience, or they may need help.

In my MBA class, the subject Organizational Behavior taught us one way of problem solving in the following sequence:

1. Identify the problem,

2. Brainstorm for some alternatives and label them: alternative 1, alternative 2, and so forth or plan A, Plan B...,

3. Once the alternatives are reached, then we have to start analyzing each for advantages and disadvantages or the cost-benefit analysis based on the data provided or gathered,

4. The alternative with higher benefit or advantages will be the basis for action,

5. Then, the strategy-creation follows. And finally, the implementation. It ends with evaluation, and the cycle begins again in a spiral manner.

Such a procedure is perfect, especially for school works and perhaps in a collective teamwork in the workplace, but it doesn't work for me in my personal level. What about my impulsive nature? What about my spontaneity? What about my temper? What about my human side? And so forth. I am aware that I can only be effectively and efficiently doing something if all my energy is focused on it. To succeed on any endeavor depends so much on the unique self-expression. What matters so much and is worth dying for one person may mean nothing to another.

My Unique Way (Outside the Box Way)

I know myself and I am very much aware of what pleases me or what triggers my "tornado-ic" tantrum to explode. Yes, I know that I should have more patience and tolerance, but I know by experience that the more I suppress my emotions, the more damaging the explosion once it eventually goes off-balance. It's an individuality thing, and I am the only person who can do something about "me." When I sense problems or problematic situations on my horizon, these are the things I do:

1. I examine the validity of the problem or situation. Is it a real or imaginary problem? Is it people around me that cause it? Is it something I caused or "invited" unknowingly to happen? Or is it just something I dream of and so desire to happen and possess but impossible to manifest at a given moment?

2. I do some brainstorming by enumerating or sketching those things that irritate me and are unacceptable to my standard.

3. Then I allow myself to get angry, really angry, even cry or wail, but I do this in the secrecy of my room or where no one would be hurt; unless, in some if not many of the occasions, I lash at the person who caused the problem. (I don't recommend this for this boomerangs.)

4. Once the emotion is out (of course I get tired too), then I naturally calm down and do meditation and introspection. In my meditation, I visualize the situation clearly enough to see the root of the problem, the symptoms, and the result, if left to flourish.

5. Once I am clear with the problem, then I create a mental scenario of the solution. Once I see and am convinced of the possibility of the ideal scene that I visualize, then I focus on it in great detail in the spirit of fun.

6. I draw the desired result from my imagination. Simulating the desired result when the problem is gone through pictures, scrapbooks, drawings, collage, and posters.

7. When my work is done, I feel amazingly at peace with myself. I even congratulate myself for having my work done. The feeling of fulfillment for being in control of my destiny is overwhelming.

My peers say I am weird, but this is how I do it and have lived my life ever since. I won't say it works for everybody, but it does work for me. Find what works for you in the personal level and create a method from that.

Four Tips to Invoke Peace into Our Lives

February 1, 2017

PEACE IS A GIFT AND a natural reward for those who seek it and work for it. We are all fallible; no matter how hard we try we still make mistakes. We stumble and we fall once in a while. When our lives become chaotic in all areas because of our own doings, whether consciously or not, then it is very difficult to live in peace from within and in our outward reality. The majority of people will just continue to live a troubled life. The areas of life that are mostly hit are relationships, health, finances, job, and unfulfilled dreams. When these happen, then that is the time we sit down and look into ourselves and investigate the motives of our hearts for the decisions and actions we have done; we do this in the spirit of compassion to ourselves instead of blaming ourselves or others or any other situations. The adage "what you sow is what you reap" is worth giving importance for introspection. There are four areas that need attention and nurturing to invite peace into our lives: 1) self-awareness, 2) environmental awareness, 3) service orientation to mankind, and 4) Godliness or the acknowledgment of a Higher Power

Self-Awareness

Rene Descartes' Cogito ergo sum (I think therefore I am) is the foundation for self-awareness. What we think is what we are. Whatever the dominating thoughts are that we harbor in our moment-by-moment life is what we become; therefore, it is what we are. In this sense, it is important that we know what we are keeping inside our minds. We have to be aware of our responses to any given stimulus in our environment because by doing so we will also discover from within ourselves what make us angry, sad, happy, jealous, and the like. This sounds simple but this is a lifetime effort if we are sincere in our pursuit for peace. We should pay attention to our emotions because these are forces within us that make or break us. It could leave a lifetime scar on our character and block us from progress in our endeavors. We often make impulsive decisions in a given moment that we feel sorry about afterward. Emotions cannot be taken for granted. Emotional responses are products of how our minds work and react to any situation, people, and objects in a given time and place. How our minds work also affects our enthusiasm, which is necessary to keep us going. Our mental attitudes are fuels to keep our desires burning for a better and meaningful life.

Environmental Awareness

Our self-awareness naturally flows toward the awareness in our environment. The American saying that goes "There are three kinds of people: those who make things happen, those who watch things happen, and those who don't know what's happening" is a perfect picture of environmental awareness. Our self-awareness will lead us to be aware of what is going on in our society. Once we know our strength and limitations, we will have a change of outlook toward the society we are in. We will be able to see and understand what people do and why people do what they do. We will be aware of the human ecology, the natural environment, the biological environment, and so forth. We will learn to connect ourselves with everything around us. We will have the feeling of belonging and oneness with the community. We will have a new understanding of human needs and human activities to improve the life condition. Relationships with love ones, neighbors, colleagues, the community, objects, material possessions, money, and the like are now in their proper perspective. Those who need to be discarded because they just unnecessarily entangled us will just vanish naturally. But this can only effectively happen after meeting the prerequisite of self-awareness.

Service Orientation

This is the stage of unfolding to the personal purpose of our existence into this life. After perfecting self-awareness and being aware of the environment, having defined our role and relationship with the society collectively, we then continue to unfold and to see what kind of service we can offer not only to our domicile but to the world as a whole. This is different from the service orientation principle in technology, but it is an application to ourselves with the same principle of offering our service to the world efficiently.

Godliness

This is the acknowledgment and connectivity to a Higher Power. There is a Great Intelligence that is the Source and the Force that governs everything that exists, natural or man-made, in the universe. I won't discuss this issue further; take it or leave it. But those who have personal experiences with the Higher Power are the ones who can attest to its role in making their lives meaningful. Lucky are they. It's like experiencing falling in love. When you describe your feelings of love to someone who has never fallen in love, or worse, doesn't believe in love, he would think you are "corny" or insane. Personal experience with "God" is just like that; it's wonderful. Try it then you will know what peace is.

A Meditation Practice

February 2, 2017

WHAT IS MEDITATION AND WHY do we need it? Meditation is paying attention to your inner and Higher Self. It is prayer in a meditative form. It is your way to self-awareness, to know what goes within you. It is common knowledge that human beings are not just bodies; we have souls and spirits. If we take care of our physical health by nourishing our bodies with healthy food, it is also equally important to nourish our souls and spirits. Knowing our desires, our inner strengths, and weaknesses is prerequisite to a healthy living, abundant life in all areas, peace, and complete happiness.

Meditation is emptying the mind, body, and heart from any concerns in your material world. This is the time to invoke your Higher Self to take charge of your life, especially when you have done all the logical thinking and nothing happens.

Following are the basics of all my meditation practices:

- I go to a quite place alone. I sit in a lotus position or lie down in silence. I breath rhythmically as I slowly close my eyes. I am now relaxing my body and my mind. I am now aware of my slowing pulse beats, unwinding and relaxing more and more in each rhythmic breath. I am now one with myself. It's only me, my life and nothing else.

- My body is now feeling lighter and lighter. A Light appears inside my forehead between my brows. It is moving fast, changing forms from tiny dots to spirals of smoke to triangles, shadows, brightness, and various colors traversing and mixing to create forms. Then some specific forms appear like clear photographs of places, people, events, and objects. I just watch them; I am detached, no feelings, no interpretations, just watch as I continue to relax with my slow breath.

- Gradually and tenderly, I focus my mind to things that I want to see and do, observing my feelings, some feelings of delight and desires. Then the visions appear just as I want them to be. Feelings of love, beauty, admiration, and joy gradually enfold me. I am now deep within my soul, to the core and nucleus of my existence, meeting my Higher Self and the Divine within me, awaiting the Divine Guidance and Message. I am now connected to the Source of all Life; I am one with the Universe. Divine Light is guiding me now. I am now attuned to the Divine Plan of my life. Divine Love is opening the way for me; He is showing me the way now. He walks before me and leads me on. He is now creating miracles in my mind, in my body, and in all my affairs.

- Now I am enjoying the beauty of nature, including me. I now see and feel the beauty of life within me. My life is precious along with the rest of all creations. I am one with the Light; I feel God's overflowing love for me. All the love I need is already within my own heart. I now share it with everyone. Everything that I need to sustain my precious life and to make my life full of bliss that I can channel to everyone concerned is already within me and will manifest in my material plane in perfect timing.

- I now open my eyes and I m wide awake, to the material plane of my existence. I feel so refreshed from that journey within me. The Higher part of me where I draw my strength for my everyday life. I am strong knowing that deep within me is the source of what I manifested in the material world; I have the balance and equilibrium of my consciousness as I live my life along with all creatures in this universe. I know that God's Will works powerfully in my life. I now accept and receive my blessings and share them with all, for the highest good of all concerned. So be it. So it is.

What to Do When Your Most Cherished Dream Fails

February 3, 2017

A DREAM COME TRUE IS a solidification of a dominating thought.

Given the premise that our mind continues working for as long as we live, whether or not we are aware of it, and that millions of fleeting thoughts pass our minds in every given moment, we should be serious in knowing what those thoughts could be. Thoughts are things; every dominating thought solidifies and becomes a reality in our material existence. The mind is creating a thought pattern unique to the individual. This thought pattern becomes the controlling mechanism in the individual's material life. This pattern that the mind creates is based on the accumulated previous experiences that is incorporated in the material reality of an individual's experiences in the present. Every experience that a person lives in his present life is an evolution of the spiraling pattern that his mind had created.

Thoughts are things. To know what kind of thoughts run through your mind, you should find a peaceful place where you cannot be distracted by any outward disturbances such as noise, other people, and happenings in your surroundings. Take a breath and tell yourself to relax and be calm and bring yourself, your mind specifically, into a sort of a trance. Close your eyes and pose a question to yourself: what do I want to do now? Or any other questions that you need some concrete answers about.

Stay calm for some minutes and "watch and listen" to the thoughts that come along. Do this like you are on top of a bridge overlooking a wide river with various small boats of varied colors floating and passing by. Listen and see your thoughts in this manner without giving inner comments or what we call mental chatters, just watch. What could happen is that the answer to your question will "speak loud and clear" as compared to those thoughts that have nothing to do with your question. The answer does not necessarily come as words; it can be a sense feeling or a gut feeling so to speak. You will have this feeling of contentment once the answer is revealed to you, and then you can come back to your normal state of mind feeling refreshed, as if something wonderful has already happened in your life. Once you are back to the normal way of thinking, you can begin doing whatever it is that you normally do, or if you remember what you "saw" in your "trance" you can jot it down or perhaps draw or sketch it. But if not, then you don't have to worry about it; the perfect time will come for the answer. Just go about your chores or normal routine. I know this is easier said than done; constant practice, though, makes perfect. You have to practice this "knowing our thoughts" exercise at least for twenty-one days. Who will pay attention to you and give importance to your thoughts more than you can do yourself? Besides, remember the premise: "Dominating thoughts are things." These are thoughts that recur and would repeatedly control our behavior and attitude toward the world around us. How our dreams came to be. The five senses and the physical world in our immediate environment and culture, plus the individual inherent perception and inclination combined, play the major role in the creation of a dream.

Let's say for example you grow up in a family of educated and talented people and your neighborhood and peer group have a similar status. All these, among any other complex situations in the sociology-demographic-economic setup, are important foundations and backgrounds that one can base the dream on. What you see, smell, touch, hear, and taste that appeal in an intensified degree are components of the kind of dream you will create and cherish, and this is not yet including the intangible things that appeal to you. In other words, the five senses are the pillars of the gateway toward "the dreamland" of your choice. This dream is then intensified by your desire or the emotions you attached to such a dream. The objective of the dream is to meet or fill the inherent vacuum that exists within every human being. Once the dream is established, the dreamer would then formulate some plans and strategies to follow and implement toward the achievement or manifestation of the dream. The existing dream now becomes the dominating thought. The dreamer would then see everything in the surrounding in terms of the dream or the dominating thought he carries within him. The picture is showing a girl who is dreaming to ride on horseback. It is the biggest thought that seems almost visible to her. When she sees a horse, she is reminded of seeing herself riding on it and she is elated with just the thought of it. She also writes about how it would feel when she actually rides on horseback. Perhaps her toys would be a toy horse and a girl riding on it, and she imagines that girl as herself. She would also collect pictures of horses; she is inclined to be attracted to anything pertaining to horse riding. All these thoughts come to her naturally until one day, she is finally able to ride on a horse in her real and material environment.

What if after doing everything, you still fail to manifest your dream to material reality? Knowing how the mind works, there are three basic things to do: 1) Clearing the mind, 2) Intensify the focus to the dominating thoughts, and 3) Wait for the perfect idea or timing and act on it once it comes to you.

Clearing the mind. The objective here is to have clarity of intention. There are many techniques to clear the mind; one is to confront your fears. By this, use the technique of posing a question to yourself, looking inside you, and asking yourself what blocks you from achieving that dream. The answer will come to you in perfect timing. Normally, what is going to happen is you will be guided to forgive yourself and others who have hurt you. This issue must be cleared; otherwise, this will cause you negative thoughts and feelings. Hence, clearing is to be aware of your negative thoughts and let them be dissolved so that only beautiful and happy thoughts will dominate your mind.

Intensify the focus to the dominating thoughts or the dream. Once clarity is achieved, you can now reinforce the focus to the dream. Whatever that dream may be, to focus is to affirm it in writing, in the form of an affirmation. An affirmation is a positive statement for that dream, such as "I am now a successful businessman." Write this statement in first, second, and third person, mentioning your name in each format. Refer to the book by Shakti Gawain entitled *Creative Visualization* for further instruction on creative visualization. Another technique is the collage making. In this, you make a collage with your picture in the center and the dream surrounding you.

Wait for the perfect idea or timing and act on it once it comes to you. There is always a perfect idea and timing for every dream to come true. What is important is we learn to relax and listen to ourselves. Always pay attention to the dominating thoughts that flow in your mind. To wait is to persist while you continue to clear the mind and to focus on the dream using simple and easy techniques. Once the idea comes, act on it.

I recommend more readings on the techniques on clearing the mind and focusing on the dominating thoughts or dreams. There are many books concerning these techniques.

Assertiveness and Self-Evaluation;
It's Not on "What" Is Said, but on "Who" Said So.

February 4, 2017

What Is Assertiveness?

The Wikipidia definition of assertiveness is "a form of behavior characterized by a confident declaration or affirmation of a statement without need of proof; this affirms the person's rights or point of view without either aggressively threatening the rights of another (assuming a position of dominance) or submissively permitting another to ignore or deny one's rights or point of view."[1]

Who is in authority to assert his person? The doctor or the ten fools combined who have never gone to any formal medical studies, and who claim they have done some research work on the field that the doctor specialized in for years via research, studies, and scientific experiments? Who has the authority? Who will you listen to? Who is more reliable? Only fools listen to hearsay and gossips because they are gullible. In this situation, one person (the doctor) is the majority against the ten unreliable fools. Any sensible person who is sick will consult with the doctor rather than listen to ten fools in the street who say that they

---

1. Wikipedia, "assertiveness," accessed April 11, 2017, https://en.wikipedia.org/wiki/Assertiveness

"researched" on your type of illness and then tell you what to do. The doctor has spent years of his life specializing in the field of medicine and the human physical condition; he did not "just research" one short time and apply his erroneous and illogical perception based on trial and error. Someone here said that one has to be nice in order to gather followers, and that's the way it is. Yes, that's the way it is in the minds of the fools but not in "high places."

The king declares one word and everyone bows before him. He is wise and no one can question his authority but a fool.

Assertiveness is not on "what" is said but "who" said so. Everybody wants to be heard, to be read, to gather a big audience to pay attention to what they say, but fools only have fools like them to listen to. The sage, the king, and the wise men won't listen to what fools say. But the fools are obliged to listen to the king no matter whether they understand what he says or not. If they don't understand, they will be beheaded without them even knowing why. And if they pay attention and understand and follow with understanding, they might be spared from the king's wrath or even be rewarded; who knows what the king might do.

The Fool Who Craves Attention Among the Masses of Fools

An extreme example or emphasis is: Proverbs 14:12 KJV

"There is a way that seems right unto a man but the end thereof is death," the wise man said. The fool gathers unto himself all the nations to support his big mouth, to shout with him in the street for their demands to be met and for their rights. The masses of fools support him and they march in the street, but there's only just one king to sign his name and say, "Banish them from my sight," and they all perish.

What do fools talk about? Fools talk about mundane everyday things, such as objects, material things, incidents, happenings, news, opinions on what they observe, how to do things, how to follow people, what other people are doing, where people are going, etc. They make big deals on all these subject matters and live all their lives getting busy on all these things.

What do assertive people talk about? Assertive people talk about "cause and effect" and wisdom. Their lives are models and examples to prove their points. They analyze things logically in terms of established facts. They don't even talk much about anything else; they just live their principled life and let things and people be. He, the assertive person, only speaks of wisdom because people consult him on why he lives life easily. He never causes problems in order to create solutions because in the first place he knows what is right and he knows that when problems come, they resolve themselves and life supports itself. In short, an assertive person is one against the majority, the gullible majority that is the target of the business world. This majority is on the bandwagon of fools who make big deals on mundane products so the inventors and the business icons who are experts in the field of human behavior create certain types of cravings and hunger in the foolish majority to believe in their needs and must patronize anything new because these are big deals to them. The majority of fools work hard for money and yet give away all their money to everything useless but it's no big deal for them because they have been "bullied" and bought into the foolish ideas. They have no idea how foolish they are. Being a fool is lots of fun for as long as they can meet all the foolish requirements. But the assertive person just watches them; he may try to warn them of the truth that only he can see, but the fools mock him because it is beyond them to see in the eyes of wisdom. They are fools, what do you expect? But what is sad is that they are the majority.

Greater Than You Can Imagine

February 5, 2017

FOLLOWING ARE TWO SHORT POEMS to remind ourselves that envy and jealousy have no place in our minds, in our hearts, and in our lives if we keep on dreaming and living our dreams. These poems are self-reminders that there is something for each of us in this universe and that each of us vary in perfect timing depending on individual differences in all our personality makeup. We are all here for good reasons; let's just live our lives and enjoy what the universe has granted us in our every here and now.

Greater Than You Can Imagine

Life is full of intervals and paradoxes;
Now you are on top, tomorrow where could you be?
It's maybe a dark night for me;
But for sure I live to welcome the new day.
You showed me your huge bank balance, your valuable possessions
 and top achievements;
Your regal mansion, jewelry, yacht, helicopters, jaguars, Cadillac,
 medals, and trophies;
All these to spite me because you see my deprivation as mediocrity.

If I am short of intuition, insight, and foresight I would have knelt
down before you in awe, adoration or perhaps envy and jealousy
with such self-pity.

But I am sorry to disappoint you because I know something that is
greater than you can imagine.

It is powerful, it lives, lives within me and we have such intimacy,
which assures me of my own greatness, the greatness that is
higher and loftier than what you can show me.

I have dreams and desires awaiting manifestations in perfect timing.

This universe has riches great enough for everyone to partake and enjoy.

I have just discovered self-awareness and the Source of wealth that
come to me in manifold.

I have just experienced the Oneness with the Mind that is Greater
than you can Imagine.

Awake My Beloved

Awake my Beloved!
It's been so long in the slumber-land;
Stretch your strong muscles now;
Stand tall and run the race before you!
The goal is just a few steps away;
Move on and reach your Mega Star;
Deep within me you've been dormant;
the loudest gongs had been sounded;
I am eager as before to watch again your achievements;
Show off your magnificence!
Reign victorious for the rest of your days.
Remember your greatness!
Awake now for Life's sake!

Perfect Timing

February 6, 2017

One of Those Things I Consider a Miracle in My Life

"If it's for you, then there is always a way." It was seven o'clock on one of those beautiful and warm mornings in the month of July 1987. But I woke up sobbing impishly as I was still lying, curling and hugging a pillow instead of my husband, who was now lying flat on his back, still sleeping; my back was on him. He was awakened by my silent sobs. He turned to me and hugged me tenderly, trying to comfort me as he asked anxiously for the reasons of my emotional state. I told him the reasons, which made him say, "If it's for you, then there is always a way." This statement of my husband reminded me of the affirmation I made to myself sometime back which says; "God reaches out for people...who can help and prosper me."

That's the wonder of growing up in a family full of love and faith; anything spiritual comes handy to believe, and that's all that matters in life: BELIEVE. And I remember what the Bible says in Matthew 9:29 KJV "According to your faith let it be done to you"...things befall you in perfect order. My ex-husband may have been a womanizer beyond my knowledge at the time, but he was an excellent husband and father to our two kids. His statement, "If it's for you, then there is always a way" was actually enough for me to dry my tears and to start my day right.

At eleven o'clock that morning, after the usual chores, breakfast, children, maids, and all, my husband told me to go to the mall to buy him some hair dye, by which I was going to dye his hair when I got back; he also said that I could not use our car since my driver was on leave for that day. So I commuted by a passenger jeepney. I was just wearing my house-dress and slippers, not taking care so much with my looks. Admittedly, my heart was still heavy that day, feeling like my life was at a dead end.

The Story Behind My Sad Emotional State

What actually caused my emotional state was my application for a teaching job in the Department of Education Culture and Sports at the Iligan City Division. I was already teaching in Iligan City Technical Institute, but I resigned because I wanted to teach in a government school. It had been three months since I submitted my application and supporting documents. Plus, there was a month of rigid interviews and examinations. There were 250 teacher applicants that summer, and after the interviews and exams, the results were evaluated and ranked. I was very excited when I saw my name ranked number 3 out of all the 250 applicants. This meant that if there were three vacant positions, one would surely be mine. But yesterday, when I dropped by the division, I saw the post: "No Vacancy." I could not help but cry since then. Actually, as far as my husband was concerned, he preferred me not to work. I didn't really have to work if that was just for money, but I would feel useless if I didn't. What a waste of my education and degree if I just stayed idle; besides, I loved teaching and I wanted to do it in a public school.

Was It Coincidence?

Back to my experience that day. After I bought the only item, the hair dye, I hailed another jeepney going home. The city was very busy with the traffic, and the sun was very hot. I was fidgety and boiling inside.

I hated the situation and the commotion of people going back and forth. I wanted to get home quickly before I yelled at the jeepney driver who was driving so slow. I was already in this depressed emotional state when suddenly, the engine of the jeepney died and everybody was sighing and murmuring because it was rush hour, and most jeepneys were full. The driver tried many times to restart the engine, but it just wouldn't work, and the passengers were becoming so restless that he ordered everybody to get down and find another jeepney because he would have his jeepney towed to the shop. This really made me angry. I yelled at the driver and cursed at him. Everybody, including the driver, quickly left the scene and I found myself left alone on that side of the road. I was standing there a while, trying to calm down myself when I realized that I was standing across the street from the division building. This made me even more depressed, seeing the big "No Vacancy" still posted there. The sun was so hot so I decided to cross the road, and once there I unthinkingly climbed up the stairs. It was already noon and most of the employees had gone home. I saw through the glass wall two supervisors getting ready to leave. Then I heard some w omen's voices coming out from the lady's room. They were complaining, and I heard one said, "There were three vacant items in Suarez High School, but the two were given away, one to the daughter of the regional supervisor and the other to…there is still one vacant position. They just keep it from those who are in the rank. They want some money for it." When I heard the words *Suarez High School*, it reminded me of Mrs. Giner, my co-church member in the Southern Baptist Church. I remember she was teaching there. After hearing that, I wasted no time. I went down the stairway and, as if intentional, a jeepney stopped right in front of me where the conductor was yelling out, "Suarez, one more passenger!" I took the jeepney and proceeded to see Ma'am Giner in Suarez High School; it was my first time going there.

I came home at two o'clock with a big grin on my face; my husband was confused. He wanted to ask why I was late but decided to leave me in my mood. For me, it was a secret that would come out when I was finally granted the appointment days later. One week later, I was the new teacher to occupy the last vacant item for that year. When something is intended by the universe for you, everything will just be easy because everything works together for good, for your success. Even the universe will bow down to your will. Isn't it a miracle?

Order of Life

February 7, 2017

LIFE EVOLVES GOING THROUGH VARIOUS stages of development. Human beings differ in development and success depending on the culture and nature of each individual. You can see for example in the development of babies, some babies start walking at six months, eight months, ten months, or one year. Not all babies start walking at the same age. Even with speaking, some speak earlier while others speak in a very later stage of development. There is a certain order and stage of development that we follow in the individual differences of development. Nature hates uniformity. Nature is all beauty and it advocates variation and harmony in its midst. There is variation and harmony in the order of life as determined by nature; hence, one cannot envy the success of another in certain areas of life even when he fails in the same area because we all differ in everything, especially in our perception of things around us and on certain inner developments.

Following is a poem that shows people's shortsightedness in this natural order of life.

Order of Life

You keep running here and there;

You are not even chasing rainbows;

You run without a direction, you just spin 'round and 'round;

You fear your shadow; it follows you wherever you are;

And so you run as fast as you can and as far can be;

You stumbled, collapsed then awakened;

 Only to continue running 'round and 'round once more.

You run away again from your own shadow, wondering why it sticks
with you, the one that you fear most.

You run to the broad light of day but you see nothing;

Except the monstrous shadow that the light creates;

You take shield in darkness for the shadow to disappear;

But the cold and chill paralyze your marrows;

Even your scream won't let out from your frozen throat;

Choked by the endless darkness in the night of your life.

The cares of life overwhelm you;

Anxiety grips your core;

Your mind is numbed and cloudy;

So you lock yourself into the darkest corner of your existence;

As you turn away from your truth, then you close your eyes in order
to forget;

Oh feeble mind, when will you come to terms with yourself?

Don't you ever realize that the shadow has no essence and is powerless
to destroy you?

Why are you hiding in that cloak and facade of retardation?

Shadows are there to announce the exact time of day, and to urge
you to move on to a sure destination.

Stop making them a monster, thus keeping you away from your
unfolding truth;

Welcome the world of colors, shapes, clarity, and natural beauty.

Stop running to and fro;

Think and be reasonable;

What are your desires?

Know yourself and start from there;

Accept your truth and let it unfold in its own phase;

Create the life you contemplate and focus on it;

Think. Think. Think.

Think on how you can achieve your dreams. Look around and look
good!

Look for the materials and tools to build your dream;

This world is in abundance to meet your every need.

Just look and see;

Look up to your star;

Look up to the sun of your existence;

It gives you the brightest light that even the shadow cannot persist.

The energy from the sun makes everything possible for you; feel it,
know it, embrace it;

The darkness is made for you to rest;

Sleep peacefully in the night, and work joyfully during the day;

Only then could you have a balanced life;

If you follow the order that your life should be.

Just a Passerby

February 8, 2017

"This World Is Not My Home."

I consider myself lucky or blessed for so many reasons. I can count my blessings, but that's beside the point. In my childhood, and before age fifteen, I was "exiled" to become a missionary. My family, consisting of Dad, Mum, sister Leah, and brother Jun, spent at least one month of summer vacation at the farm every year. Our farm was called Chile Valley, to honor Brother Raul Escobar from Chile.

He was the first missionary of the International Missionary Society to come to the Philippines and who converted my dad to become a missionary himself. My dad was one of the two pioneering Filipino missionaries under this organization. The foreigner missionaries, such as Andrade, Pizzarro, Abraham, Nicolicci, Kozel, among others, frequented our beautiful farm, and I grew up mingling with them. Being the eldest child, I was the center of attention to my dad's frequent visitors and colleagues; he bragged about me to them, not that I was happy about that. I was made to recite three chapters of Bible verses to the missionaries, and a lot more show-offs about me as presented by my dad to his comrades. In our family worship hour, done twice a day at 5:00 to 6:00 a.m. and 5:00 to 6:00 p.m., my dad would lead us in singing "This world is not my home I am just passing by..." and "I am a stranger here within a foreign land, my home is far away upon the golden strand; Ambassador to be in realms beyond the sea, I'm here on business for my King."

While I was far from home being in the IMS (International Missionary Society) in Manila as a colporteur, my dad also started his "nomadic" life, bringing along my siblings and mum, as they were assigned to several places around the country as a missionary family. One of my dad's favorite verses from the Bible is found in Luke 14:26, which he often recited to us every worship time, and has a message to the effect "Those who cannot leave his land, house, family, in my name are not worthy of me, cannot be my disciple..." I learned to hate this verse. Because of my dad's fanatic conversion, he distributed his land to thirty poor families and left only a six-hectare parcel of farm, which he entrusted to his brother Tirso, who, himself had a ten-hectare farm of his own. He also sold our two houses in the city, and then joined the missionary work as a volunteer. When I came home from missionary work, I was met by a very different home life situation. Gone were the comforts of home, and I found my family living in my uncle's house.

"This Too Will Pass."

That background of my life has long passed, and I am in my "here and now." The shoes I wore when I was six years old, even if they were still good and usable, I could not wear them now that I am sixty-two. We change along with the passing of time, not just physically but also intellectually; otherwise, we would be intellectual "bonsai."

We change not only physically but also intellectually and in our value systems, viewpoints, and core beliefs. What I used to believe when I was fifteen years old and was with my family is not what I believe now. We change our belief systems; otherwise, we would just be beautiful but callous and empty-headed mannequins.

Everything that we have been through has passed away as we continue to live and evolve until our time will come to pass away too. We all have been through a lot of situations in life; some situations call for celebrations and are full of excitement, other situations are sadness and loss but they all pass away. Some experiences make us honorable and dignified, while others are embarrassing and a disgrace. These are experiences in life that all pass by. Some friends and loved ones leave this life ahead of us. They have experienced lots of happiness and joy in this life. They possessed material goods and achieved success in their own rights. They also experienced a lot of problems that sometimes, if not often, seemed unbearable, but everything passes by including each of them.

Living in My "Here And Now"

A phrase from the poem, "The Miller of the Dee" I quote, "...I envy nobody and nobody envies me..." is worth pondering. If we live in the "here and now," life could be meaningful and worth living. What are the things to do in the "here and now" that can make life meaningful? Living in the here and now means appreciating our value as people in a moment-by-moment basis. All things come and go, all experiences pass by, people come and and people go, but nobody stays with us permanently, even our own children.

Then what is left with us? With you? My good friend and colleague, Ma'am Semeramis Bamba, died of lung cancer years back; she was just fifty. She was five years younger than me. She was a brilliant English professor. She had everything: two beautiful grandchildren, three beautiful and educated daughters, a prestigious position in school...the list could go on. She never smoked, was a perfectionist in all her ways, and she was near to perfection in her looks and beauty. Such a waste for a brilliant and beautiful human. Two days before she died, Ma'am

Veron and I visited her in the hospital, and her last words to us, to me specifically, were,

"Ma'am Jenny, you are one of my sources of inspiration when something confuses me...but you smoke and never had cancer, whereas I am careful in my food and I never smoke but look at me. You are carefree, you get angry when you want, you laugh when you feel good, you have the presence of mind, and an assertiveness that anyone can wonder. You love and you are loved...you never suppress your emotions and that makes you significant from the rest of us...I wish I could turn back the time so I can live in my here and now full of freedom rather than full of restrictions and plans that never work."

I never realized how I scored with my colleagues except from the mouth of a dying dear friend. I consider life as just a dream. My every here and now is a dream. Today is the manifestation of what I dreamed yesterday. I don't know exactly what tomorrow is, but I know that the beautiful dream I dream today is the beautiful tomorrow that will come my way. So, my here and now is a beautiful dream. That kind of dream that will be my tomorrow's here and now. Like everybody else, I am just a passerby in this life, the life that is just a dream, like a dream that fades like bubbles. It is what life and everything in it is all about.

Choose to Remember

February 9, 2017

EVERY PERSON ALIVE HAS BEEN through a lot of ups and downs and twists and turns in life; no one is exempted. No matter how careful a person is, there is always a time in his life that he feels sad and empty. Those we see as being happy and in great abundance and looking loved and cared for in a given time must have also experienced some low points in life in the past. Whether real or perceived or imaginary, these low points are real for the person in question. No one is exempted because life is movement and development, even if we want to believe that there is stability if we just follow the rules. The rule is "CHANGE" and "MOVEMENT," but then we don't have to panic because we are also equipped with antidotes to counter and to straighten every turn that happens in our lives. All we need to do is to summon these tools to your rescue and protection in order to survive and to continue moving on. The fact is everything passes: sadness, happiness, grief, even abundance. When you are at the top you can expect to fall by a single wrong step, but that's not the end unless you die by that fall. That is the reason why we have to celebrate life because life means continuous movement toward your destiny while you still have it.

During one of those low times of my life, I wrote a poem to remind me that it was not the end of the world for me. I was still alive and I had gone a long way since then.

Language of My Soul at the Time

My New Zealander husband, Adrian Shiels, died in 2003, but he had been bedridden for two years till the end. I wrote the following narrative to myself on January 4, 2001 when I had to quit my job to take care of him. It was among the lowest points of my life, and I felt so isolated considering the many years I spent in the academe as a professor, in my masters studies and other social activities. I share it here in a narrative poetic form to remind everyone that life has twists beyond human control regardless of the best efforts we offer for its enjoyment and success. This poem is also a reminder that we have to embrace life, including the pain and the sorrows that may pass our way. Each person must be the number one fan and lover of himself; otherwise, who else will?

Choose to Remember

Why are you so sad my dearest?
You look so awful;
You don't take a bath;
You don't comb your hair;
You don't wash your face;
Your dirty and skinny face sags;
You don't even change your clothes for many days;
Look in the mirror, your sunken eyes are fixed to nowhere, your
    brows meet, your forehead wrinkles, you look a century older;
Your lips are pouting and dry; have you anything for your stomach yet?
Is this how you want yourself to look?
Why do you brood and sulk?
Sitting down in the dark corner of this cold room with bowed head
    and drooping shoulders;
Bent long knees reaching above your head;

How long have you been in this condition? Days? Months? Years?

You don't go out anymore like you used to do; you don't talk to
people who are more in need for your words of comfort;

You are so dysfunctional even for your personal well-being.

What is the big deal?

Is it because you believe that nobody cares for you?

Is it because you are convinced that nobody remembers you?

Is it a feeling of rejection?

Is it deprivation of material possessions?

Or is it a belief that you are a failure or a loser in life?

Is it a feeling that you are at a dead-end in life's journey?

What exactly is it that brought you to this miserable state?

That you just have to drift to nothingness making your life worthless
in the process?

Do you feel that all your dreams and wishes have turned to ashes?

Now, my Beloved, take a long deep breath;

Listen to my counsel once and for all.

You still have the mind; it's your tool to remember what you really
are, a tool to lift you up from misery; use it if it's just for now.

Remember how you used to be; how you always are yesterday, today,
and through eternity;

Recall what you used to teach me on life's reality.

Do you remember who you are?

Remember your natural state of being;

"I am a survivor" remember saying this?

Remember you are an asset, a treasure and a joy to those around you?

Remember your inheritance?

Remember your true love? Your feelings of love?

Remember who loves you with such unconditional love?

Remember He delights in serving you?

Remember he He provides everything for you "according to His riches in glory"?

Start looking at the brighter side of life.

Notice that the dark side is there to illumine the light;

Just choose to remember that the sun rises after the darkest dawn.

Remember that the most powerful weapon against darkness is to shine.

Fear not the shadows, don't let them bother you, never allow them to pull you down, use them as your footstool instead to catapult you to the brightest star above.

Arise now My Beloved!

Clean up and purge yourself.

Choose gladness and a merry heart; whistle a tune or two if you must.

Choose wisdom and discernment.

Reenlist and summon your bright experiences of joy and success.

Choose love and compassion;

Choose forgiveness and peace;

Choose hope and faith;

Choose to believe;

Choose dignity, health, beauty, and prosperity;

Choose goodness and kindness;

Focus your mind to the Light within you;

Only then will the shadows disappear;

So choose to remember.

Remember now?

Sometimes, only us (you, I) can lift us up from life's miseries. Everything we need is already within us, if we just choose to remember... remember that even the darkest cloud has its silver lining.

My Invisible Little World

February 10, 2017

IN THE PAST, BEFORE PARANORMAL science announced to the world through self-help books that fantasy and imagination are good tools to keep life going, people were ashamed to even create imaginary reality that existed only in their minds. Where do all these paintings of great artists come from, and all the fantastic fairy tales? Didn't they come from richly imaginative minds of the artists and writers? Children and teenagers have very rich imaginations, and in the past many people thought that to imagine was useless and nonproductive and would brush it off as "it's just an imagination," which meant it could not come true. I read a book about imagery that tells of the relevance of imagination as having helped a person heal his illness, winning an athletic game among others. To imagine and fantasize is to help ourselves escape from the harsh reality of the present situation that castigates us in certain low times of our lives. When nothing else helps, use your imagination; it will do wonders in your life. Trust me on this.

A Narrative Poem

I wrote this narrative poem on June 2, 2002 when I was jobless, because I was care-giving full time to my then bedridden husband, Adrian Shiels. He died ten months later. I share this experience as an example of a good imagination that can help us through the darkness of our lives. In times when there is nothing you can do anymore to change your difficult situation, go deep down within you and create a beautiful world of your own. It's free to dream, and God knows what comes next. The idea is to enjoy life, even if it is only in your imagination.

My Invisible Little World

Beyond anyone else's understanding and imagination;
Lies my invisible little world.
No one can reach it; it's farther than the least visible star on a clear
    starry night;
It lies in the depths beyond the deepest ocean floor; it's nowhere even
    in the earth's core.
No one knows of its existence;
Nobody has even thought about it; if there was one to sense of its
    existence, then he must be a psychic;
Yet it does exists in anyone alive.
Isn't everybody's beliefs based on his experience?
Those that can be seen, heard, and the rest of the senses?
My invisible world is me, my mind, my emotions, and the complete
    me.
My invisible world is a perfectly beautiful and harmonious kingdom;
I am the crowned and honorable queen;
My king's throne and my own are set side by side;
My adorable king adores me as much;
We are soul mates that hail from time immemorial;
He delights in me, he loves me, he serves me, and pampers me;
My king is my life and so am I to him;
Nothing can come between us;

Death is powerless, for my king and I are inseparable.

There is love beyond compare in my invisible little world.

My invisible little world is an untouched paradise of beauty and abundance; my court servants are angels and cherubim and sage; they sing to the voice of rain and thunder a-blending; they dance with the gracefulness of the cool breeze;

They play the harp with the soothing and harmonic melodies of the rushing creek; such pleasure beyond compare in my invisible little world.

My mentors and sources of knowledge and wisdom are the wiz of the ancient worlds beyond the sky;

They tell of a land where fire and water mix;

They tell of a love, a hope, and a courage that create the universe;

They tell of alpha and omega, of unending stories of subjects beyond human discernment;

Such joy beyond compare in my invisible little world.

In my invisible little world, everybody loves everybody;

Everybody makes everybody happy;

Everybody appreciates everybody's uniqueness;

Everybody is vibrantly healthy and radiantly beautiful;

Everybody is a genius and talented;

Criticism is an alien in my invisible world;

Comparison and condemnation are outsiders;

Everybody and everything is just perfectly beautiful and harmonious.

My invisible little world is not a utopia; it's a fact;

Of course you can laugh;

How can a born-blind person understand red when all his life everything is black?

He can laugh to his heart's satisfaction, despite his predicament, if someone insists to him the existence of any color;

He cannot even understand black, even if that is his only world because color is just beyond his nature and he's got no point of comparison.

So is everybody who heard my story of my invisible little world. Did you say that I am living in fantasy?

That I am deluded or idealistic?

Whatever you call it, the fact remains that the outside world is now filled with comfort and convenience, because of the people who were once called crazy, lunatic, deluded, when they were just bringing out the existence of their invisible little world.

Try to turn the pages of history;

Read the life of the ineducable idiot Thomas Edison;

The two brothers who died and whose death contributed to make the world smaller by reaching far destinations by flying.

My invisible little world is a universe. Discover that within you, my friend. For God's sake!

Problems Resolve Themselves

February 11, 2017

Any Problem?

One hubber suggested to me that I should write articles that deal with everyday problems, such topic as "how to teach a dog to stop licking the wall." I almost laughed but I saw how serious she was, and she even added that this was the kind of hubs that earned money in Hubpages—where I was a writer and contributor. This is the kind of topic that would trigger lots of comments, appreciations, applause, and followers. She also said that I would not have traffic and followers if I didn't write like she suggested. I didn't really worry about this. If there were no people to follow me, then the angels would, or they would draw people to follow me, and if it was not in Hubpages, then who knows where it would be. The point is, I really have no problems in this area.

Be that as it may, I am just not the type of writer who can write mundane things just so I can earn and be applauded by the majority. I will just be one and won't really care if I just have one sincere and honest-to-goodness reader who learns wisdom from my writing and whose life is a bit touched and inspired by my words. In this sense, I will be very happy like I hear the hosts of angels in heaven singing. The bottom line is, I won't compromise myself and my principles in exchange for meager coins I could earn from Hubpages(if I do earn, but I am not earning so I have less worry). I don't collect pebbles; I go for gold nuggets. Do you know how much I earn if someone's heart is touched by my words? I earn the Source of Infinite abundance and can draw my money anytime I need it, not in Hubpages though. It's my secret between me and God, or the universe, or the universal law, which says "What you sow is what you reap." Every heart that is touched or inspired by reading my writings is worth a million angels singing, and the pay-off in monetary terms is enormous. Whether I do something or nothing I always have enough money to pay my bills, rent, live in a condominium with maids to attend to my needs, and a driver and car to move me around as I wish without worrying about money. Impossible? Not for me. I just touch hearts and inspire people, and my compensation is paid NATURALLY in great abundance. I can only write those things that I am truly convinced about, and I am just sharing some wisdom.

Just appreciate the beauty and abundance in life, and problems resolve themselves naturally, writing on Universal Truth rather than problems.

The statement "Problems resolve themselves" always works for me in every area of my life. How to make it work is where the efforts are concentrated. I am not very much on talking about problems or solutions; I consider problems as challenges that are fun to face like it's another adventure. Problems trigger our creative abilities. The adage, "Necessity is the mother of invention" applies, given a situation. When real problems come, then that is the time for you to draw from your "well of wisdom" or your "cabinet in the mind" what you stocked there for any contingency. The only question is, do you have enough stock (wisdom, knowledge, confidence, etc.) to counter any situation in your life? This is where we concentrate; we have to update our "stocks" so that we will always have plenty of it when the need arises.

Problems vs. Creativity

If you live your life according to your natural flow, then problems can be prevented. Life supports itself and there is actually nothing to worry about, but it is sad to note that 99.99 percent of people focus more on problems and problem solving rather than on creating, discovering, inventing, and producing. When somebody says, "I am a problem solver" or a "troubleshooter," it only means that he is an expert in causing problems in his life. People create problems at every turn; one problem generates another problem to "solve" the previous. One problem leads to another problem then to another and more and more problems over the years; hence, a person lives a life full of problems. Such a coping life.

A life of creativity is such that a person lives his life in a moment-by-moment basis; he is assertive to appreciate what is good and beautiful in everything and everyone around him while accepting and letting everything be without allowing anything "bad and ugly" to bother him. A creative mind eliminates bad thoughts naturally because it can only see the good and the beautiful, wherein it capitalizes on using these good things to improve and run his life.

I Am a Traveler

February 12, 2017

THIS POEM, WHICH I WROTE years back in Hubpages, is symbolic of a person's deep longings and on his search for happiness in this life. It is also symbolic of the nature of life, which is MOVEMENT. Life is movement, a journey and a destiny; this is what this poem is all about.

I Am a Traveler

Destiny?
From my native land I fled, to the Land of Promise beyond;
It will take me a lifetime, conditions, emotions, and lots of decision
    making before I can ever reach my destiny;
The Destiny that is drawing me closer but never arriving there.

Why must I leave?
Don't I have loved ones who gladly accommodate and cheer me?
I can choose to stay and try to feel good about it;
My native land has its own culture;
People here get along well;
There is plenty of food, drinks, jobs, abundance of love, and camaraderie;
I can live forever here and be merry for the rest of my life;

Everything I need is already here;

My native land is a wonderful place to raise a family;

A few get rich and almost everyone seems happy and contented;

The leaders who govern the masses are idolized and are the ideals of
the citizenry;

They are the law, the status quo, and the models of society;

Why can't I just stay and comply?

Who knows what comes out here for me?

But I am a traveler; my parents were too;

They just happened to make this place one of their stopovers during
my birth;

And they stayed too long, long enough for both of them to die here
and for me to forget of my true origin;

They got very busy establishing rapport with the natives here;

The inhabitants here benefited from their creativity;

They gathered treasures for themselves from the rich resources in this
God-given blessed land;

The people loved them so much;

My parents built their mansion here, and before they died they were
able to distribute their properties and share their blessings with
the peasants.

But I am a traveler, it's in my blood;

Now that I am on my own I must continue the journey that has been
long interrupted;

I have to survey the world and discover new things in different lands
and people;

That is my mission as a traveler;

I will achieve the objective of the mission that my parents had chosen
to forget;
My accomplishments, achievements, and experiences with people,
both natives and travelers, and with nature along the way;
Make my life worth living.

If I'd prefer to stay, it would only be an empty body;
Because my heart, my mind, and my soul take me to distant lands;
To be with other travelers like me;
Who always long to be home;
To be home in the Promised Land;
To be with the King of kings of my Destiny;
He is the King of the Promised Land, the King of the Ultimate
Destiny
Where everyone alive, both people and everything in this vast
universe, are destined;
I have to go ahead;
And perform my mission;
For I was born to achieve and to lighten the hearts of other travelers
Who continue searching for the meaning of life, the now and the
beyond.
My travels may be full of adventures, pleasant or unpleasant;
But my reward will be the crown from the King
Who is all-knowing and omnipotent;
This is my mission; I am a traveler.

Powerful Feelings

February 13, 2017

Feelings

Who can truly understand the feelings within me?

Can anyone see that my feelings are life itself that can control me?

My feelings are sensitive and responsive to my thoughts, perceptions, and interpretations of things around me;

My feelings react to situations, people, places, events, and conditions that surround me;

They react to temperatures, weather, and anything that can be felt or sensed.

My feelings are so delicate and tender yet also vehement and explosive;

They are the index of my very soul;

And must be guided and guarded for they are so powerful.

How I live my life and my lifestyle is the product of the moment-by-moment feelings and the feelings that I accumulate within me;

My total personality depends so much on my emotional state in a given moment;

My moment-by-moment feelings can lead to achievements or failures as the case maybe;

To creativity nd productivity or to failures and destruction depending on the feelings I constantly keep within me and express outwardly;

My feelings compel me to behave and act accordingly in a given time and place with certain conditions and people;

My beautiful and positive feelings in a given time and space, reflect to everyone around me;

Everybody would feel wonderful and life will be blessed;

But if ugly and negative feelings prevail in me for long, life for everyone, including my own and my loved ones would be miserable;

Oh, it is therefore important that my feelings must be under God's guidance and control.

Suppressing my feelings makes my life bitter and worse later;

It's like hiding rotten vegetables and dead animals in a vacuumed closet;

Where worms and maggots produce poisoned gasses and deadly odors;

To gradually consume the soul.

Even beautiful feelings, such as love and compassion, if denied due expression would be like hiding burning coals under a pile of fresh leaves and grasses inside a box of rubbish;

Soon the smoke comes out, followed by explosive heat, which eventually turns into fire and the destruction of lives around it.

When I feel very tired and confused that makes me dysfunctional;

Then I know for sure that deep within me are feelings that are ignored.

Headaches, stomachaches, body aches, and fatal diseases such as tumors and cancers can be the results of anger, resentments, frustrations, rejections, and anguish of the soul.

Worries and anxieties if not checked and resolved lead to wasted lives
and failures;

Hurting feelings such as guilt, betrayals, hatred, jealousy, envy, fear, and
inadequacy, being misunderstood and maltreated, must be faced
squarely and be brought out to its proper place and perspective;

The mind is equipped with the necessary tools to combat these dark
and destructive feelings;

Let the mind summon all its forces to blot out and dissolve these
feelings of doom.

Hurt feelings are heavy and burdensome; they wear down the soul;

But I am greater than my feelings, and even greater than my mind;

I am the master of my soul.

I have to check my feelings every now and then before they reproduce
and create a clan within me;

I have to be aware of their presence and their effects in me and on
my life as a whole;

So many lives had been destroyed by uncontrolled and unguarded feelings;

Broken homes and crimes to mention a few;

I have to scrutinize their nature until there is nothing of their sorts
left in me;

Only then can I purge myself and begin to shine.

And when the Light within me shines brightly;

The Light that emanates from the Divine Source;

All the shadows and darkness caused by hurting feelings will be gone;

I am myself once more;

I just have to acknowledge my feelings as part of me;

Select the good feelings and let them stay;

Recognize those feelings that could hurt and banish them away.

Peace, joy, hope, faith, forgiveness, and love are the only feelings that
I keep.

How to Live an Abundant Life

February 14, 2017

A Blessed Life

"Balance" is the key. I will list here the seven major ingredients for a balanced and blessed or fulfilling life:

1. Self-Expression
2. Relationships
3. Work/Job/Position/Career/Business
4. Money/Material Possessions
5. Leisure/Hobbies
6. Travels/Explorations/Growth and Development/Expansion
7. Sharing

What is within, so is without. Following are the discussions on the items listed above as components of a balanced life:

<u>Self-Expression</u>. To top the list for a balanced life is self-expression. How you live your life, your lifestyle, your relationships in all types, your career, your income, and all the rest of your life's experiences are determined by how you see and regard yourself from within as you

effectively express it to the world or the society where you belong. It is very easy to enumerate all these balancing components of a fulfilling life, but to live a balanced life starts from how you live your "inner life" and effectively present it outward. Each of us lives in our own "inner world"; this "inner world" exactly and automatically reflects on your outside world or to the circumstances in your life. Who are you in your inner world? Are you beautiful, smart, healthy, and friendly? What are the roles you play in your inner world? Are you happy with yourself? How do you dress yourself? What are the words you say to yourself? Are they encouraging words? Do you love, respect, and accept yourself just as you are and completely in your inner world? Do you see yourself as needing improvement? How do you improve yourself in your inner world? How do you see yourself interacting with people? Who are these people you include and invite to participate in all your activities and who help you develop your potentials? Do you invite only people who can prosper you? Or do you invite enemies too? These are just among the millions of situations, people, events, and life experiences that interplay as the content or inhabitants in your "inner world." Whatever is the content of your inner world—good or bad, negative or positive, happy or sad, rich or poor, the list can continue to infinity—are the ones that replicate in your outward reality. Each one's reality exists in the inside; the outside is just the mirror of such reality.

Strength in Relationship/Family Relationship/Importance of Strength in Relationships. This reminds me of the very good question of another hubber, KeithJK, which goes: "If you had a limit of seven, who would you want in your Heaven?" I answered as follows:

1. Papa for logical and intellectual outlook in life and abundance

2. Mama for unfailing love and purity of heart and intention

3. Rey (my son) for my joy and inspiration

4. Jean (my daughter) for relishing the beauty of this universe

5. Greg (my husband) for extending my desire to continue living

6. Ma'am Veron (my best friend) for being my sounding board and mirror of what is going on around me in connection to my assertiveness

7. Betty (my English ex-sister-in-law) for interracial closeness of any type of relationship

If I am not limited to seven, I have a million more people to take with me to my Heaven...for very good reasons. Given the premise of perfect self-expression that originates from your own inner world, the people, including animals or pets, and even material possessions and events in your life, are products of the quality of the inner world you have created. You are the artist who creates your inner world. You created you and everything that is you—your thoughts, your feelings, your physical looks, your activities, and the people involved in everything that is you, and a lot more than you can imagine. This time let's focus on relationships. Strength in any relationships depends so much on your own strength to deal with yourself. Whatever is the quality of your self-esteem or self-value reflects on the quality of people and strength and weakness of relationships you have with others. Let me list some basic relationships that could determine how balanced your life is:

- Family

- Peer group and friends

- Colleagues and associates

- Interaction and socialization with the general public

Family. Are you a loving, responsible, and devoted daughter/son, sister/brother, wife/husband, mother/father? Plus, all the attractive personality traits as a family member.

Peer group and friends. How do you see the immediate people around you? The quality and strength of your relationship with your family makes an impression on how your peer group and friends regard you, and in turn determines how you react with the individuality of your peers.

Colleagues and associates. If you are a responsible member of the family (depending on how you define "responsible"), then your colleagues also see you as such, and everything will be easy for you to climb the ladder of success in whatever you do or in whatever position you have in your job/business situation. Isn't that people help in many different ways, to prosper you when most, if not all of them see your integrity?

The general public. This is sometimes, if not often, a scary situation in the sense that you are a stranger or unfamiliar with the place, the people and the culture as a whole. Depending on what society you are situated or you happen to be in, the point is you have to be assertive and watchful in all your dealings. These are the people outside your safety zone, and yet, how you are in your "inner world," in your family, in your peer group, and in your associates will also determine how you handle yourself in the bigger world.

To summarize: Strength or weakness in any form of relationships is a strong determinant in the balancing of your life.

Career/Money/Work/Job/Position/Career/Business/Money/
Material Possessions. It is now easy to understand how things are related once the foundation is established. This reminds me of another hubber, dallas93444, who answered my forum, which asks, "How do you accept failure?" His perfect response was, "Failure is a definition of an event. A

'failure' can be a building block, rather than a stumbling block...We get to decide."

Most of us experience similar things; our reaction to them defines who we are... Your success depends so much on your reaction to certain events in your life. Can you see what needs improvement in your career/business, and can you determine how much money or income per any given period you are worth according to your personal assessment, personal value, and capability? These are all parts of your self-expression process in your "inner world." The strength of your relationships in all four categories also determine how far you can go because people in your circle help, in any way, to push you naturally, based on their individual connection with you in the relationship category.

Leisure/Hobbies Travels/Explorations/Growth and Development/Expansion. There is truth in the old adage: "Work and work makes one dull; work and play makes one happy." This area of a balanced life covers a wide range: travel, hobby, play and enjoy with family and loved ones, going back to school for some short or long term, additional skills and knowledge, and just being happy with the company or bonding with any or all of the four relationship categories. This includes doing what you exactly want to do as a hobby or perhaps an alternative means of earning.

Sharing the Balanced Life. There's another old adage that really works well for me and my loved ones and the whole of my relationship cycle: "You can give without loving, but you cannot love without giving."

To summarize: a balanced life is one that has abundance in joy and success in all seven areas of life—as mentioned in the onset of this discussion—and ends in sharing all of your blessings in all these areas with people around you and the next generation.

My Life Is Shaped by My Choices

February 15, 2017

LIFE IS WHAT WE MAKE it. This article is all about the decisions we make in every turn in this life. We make choices in any given situation. Life has many choices and in making those choices you need to be aware of what you really want and what you deserve in this life. Self-awareness is very important; otherwise, if you live your life depending on someone else's decisions, you won't be happy. Lots of people will come to a point where they say, "I have no choices." This is a dead-end statement; there are always many choices in life in all areas. We often make wrong decisions and make mistakes. Some mistakes are small and can easily be straightened, but some are big enough to change the direction of our lives toward more and more mistakes that make us feel like failures and useless. That is why self-awareness is very important. It guides us in the right direction so that we can acknowledge at any time that we are being sidetracked; hence, we can immediately correct our mistakes before everything is out of control. Every mistake we make has consequences that we suffer. The bigger the mistake the bigger the punishment, and these punishments cost us time and misery, if we are lucky to be still alive. To make mistakes is human, and we must not be afraid to make one. The good news is we can always choose to forgive ourselves, correct the mistake as soon as we recognize it, and then continue moving in the right direction.

Self-Awareness

My decisions are statements of my identity. Every decision I make embodies my self-concept and my view of the world. Choices are not mere isolated events on the periphery of my life; rather, choices are my life. Good decisions are my true thoughts and feelings, my beliefs and emotions that draw vital wisdom inherent in me. I am conscious of my motivations. I am aware of the beliefs that propel me toward or away from what I truly desire or my goals and dreams. I am always Divinely-guided and my spiritual awareness leads me to the fulfilling life that I deserve.

Here are two important choices you can make: chase rainbows and make goals. People are busy "chasing rainbows." What are most people busy about?

Most people are busy searching how earn more money, whether on the net or in a real-life situation. Everything they do is always a by-product of their persistence to get more money. It's not bad actually, when they do it in all honesty of intention; it is valid when they do it with integrity and without molesting or destroying other people's works and lives. I advocate Divine Guidance in securing a life of abundance rather than on the "chasing rainbows" method of acquiring wealth. Remember that the more you chase anything the faster it flees away from you. I like the lines of a song (I added more words based on my experiences): "Are you tired of chasing pretty rainbows? Are you tired of spinning round and round? Lay down your dreams and submit it to the Greatest Intelligence that knows better than you can ever know in your lifetime."

Each of us lives our lives by following certain sets of patterns that our psyches have perceived and set for us as a result of our imaginations, choices, decision making, and actual life experiences over the years. Life is so full of complexities that it is difficult to focus on a goal that we supposedly desire to achieve. In the first place, even to create a goal is complicated by itself because it needs a certain degree of conviction within us; otherwise, fear gets in the way. That fear of not achieving the goal is by itself a block to create a goal. Many people try to create a goal, but deep within them is a feeling that says, "It's just a goal. I am not 100 percent sure I can achieve it."

Dreams and Goals

What choices do you have? What are your goals?

There are as many goals as there are many needs, wants, desires, and urges on the individual level. Lots of people get mixed up in their goals for education, career, money, self-esteem, socialization, status quo, health, fitness, beauty, relationships, romance, comfort, self-actualization, and the list could go on to infinity.

Goals undergo certain processes starting from 1) why the goal was created, 2) what specific goal to focus on in a specific time and place, 3) the advantages and disadvantages of setting such a goal, 4) setting alternative courses of actions to pursue such a goal, 5) the pros and cons of a chosen alternative, and 6) strategies of implementing the chosen course of action.

These are just among other things that any sensible person can do. What about those who never bother to create a goal in the first place because they have such mental attitude as to just exist and follow whatever society is set for them? What will happen to the definition of man as a sentient being? Man as a thinking being? Even "to think" or "not to think" is a matter of choice. "To think" is to set goals for one's self in any area of one's existence. "Not to think" means, "to just drift in life wherever it may lead him and to follow what everybody else thinks and does. It's easier to imitate or duplicate than to design, create, and be original.

Given these two choices—chasing rainbows and creating goals—which would you prefer?

Writing Affirmations

February 16, 2017

AFFIRMATIONS ARE THE WORDS WE say to ourselves repeatedly every day and whenever we have the chance. Inside our minds are many clatters that we have collected from other people, including parents, family members, friends, observations in our environment, the media, and what we read and studied in school. This is the very reason why I don't just collect and share quotes that many people post on Facebook that do not jibe with my own core beliefs and value system.

When you do affirmations you will notice that there are opposing clatters within you. As an example, let's say you affirm to yourself, "I, Jenny, am a millionaire." This is the right format of an affirmation. You should mention your name in three persons, the I, you, and she if you are a female, or he if you are a male. Completing the example: "You, Jenny, are a millionaire. She, Jenny, is a millionaire." To continue with my example question, what does your mind or core belief say when you say to yourself that you are a millionaire? Of course something in you would at least laugh hilariously and say, "What a joke!" Especially when you know that you don't even have enough money to buy your basic survival needs, that no matter how you work hard, money is just not enough for everything that you and your family needs. And it's even worse when you are jobless and have no regular source of income. To say it's a joke would escalate to "Are you crazy?" "You must be desperate, wake up!" "It's useless!" "Stop it!" "You're just dreaming or hallucinating. Look at your reality; it's a lie!" "It's impossible; there's no chance!" Then the feeling of desperation and worry about money follows. You feel hopeless and might even hate yourself for doing such affirmations. You feel like you are gullible to even try to follow what you just have learned. Eventually, you accept the fact that you are just poor and are not meant to live a rich life. You know deep within you that you are just fantasizing and that no matter what you do, becoming a millionaire is just so outrageously unbelievable and impossible and is just not for you unless you win the lottery, which is by itself a very slim chance. It's like hitting the moon with your own fist. This is another reason why you don't just do affirmation without prior knowledge about how affirmations work, because it may just have a reverse effect on you and cement in you the skepticism that you already had prior. Instead of making your affirmation manifest for you, it would rather make your situation worst. You have to understand the mechanics of affirmations before starting to do it. There are various types of things you affirm.

Some of those you affirm to yourself manifest instantly, as instantly as while you are still doing it, but some will take a very long time, years maybe even decades, to the point that you already forgot about it. By that time, you will have undergone so many processes and changes in your life. The reason is, it would take a lot of convincing your psyche to believe that you are serious about what you are affirming to yourself, and your mind clatters are stronger or more powerful to run your life, it had created a solid pattern in you because you had allowed it either consciously or otherwise, it's been doing that for a long time for you without you even being aware of it.

Cemented in our core belief system, which has created patterns that are difficult to change and replace, are those that were inculcated in us by our culture. Culture includes religion, family tradition, peer group orientations, and everything involved in your socialization process, plus your perception on how you react in every given situation. It's sad to say that many, if not most, of these core belief systems are destructive to the unfolding of your true destination and self. Hence, when a new idea is introduced to you it will be repulsive to your belief system if it has nothing to do with what you are familiar with. You cannot accept the fact that there are truths other than what you are used to believing. Citing my example, you are familiar with the fact that nobody can get rich—a millionaire for that matter—by mere affirmation. One has to work hard and needs ample time in order to succeed. I can feel that while I am typing this idea, those who are reading this article would say, "Of course hard work is necessary to become a millionaire, and it will take time and a lot of trial and error." I don't undermine hard work, but it has to be doing the right work for you. You can be a hardworking clerk in a small office, but such nature of work won't make you a millionaire, even if you do that till you lose your last breath. Only those driven people who work hard because they are fully convinced of their foresight, and are on the right tract to their millions, will succeed. In short, be open-minded and change your way of thinking and belief system.

So how then does affirmation work in order to manifest your desires? Aside from manifestation of what you affirmed for, I would like to cite here some good uses and advantages in doing affirmations. Habitual affirmation has healing effects, not only on the soul level but to your life as a whole. It is a good method of unfolding you toward your perfect destination in this life. It trains your mind to perceive things that are not clear to you before and to others. It is a perfect way to creativity and self-confidence. It makes you a better person, not to mention richer in every area in your life. Those are just a few of the things that doing affirmations can do to our lives.

Manifestations as Results of Affirmations

February 17, 2017

THIS IS THE CONTINUATION OF what I wrote yesterday about writing affirmations. As I said, writing affirmations already has many benefits, even before what you affirmed has manifested. I also said that some affirmations manifest instantly while some take years even decades, but the fact is whatever you affirmed to yourself will always manifest sooner or later. With written affirmations, you should do it for at least twenty-eight days. According to studies, this is the least amount of time that whatever we practice or exercise in the mental plane will take effect, although you can continue if you still want to.

I had this really unforgettable experience of manifestation as a result of my affirmation. This was one of those instant results, and it really did amaze me. That's why I advocate and encourage everybody to practice this. Doing affirmations is such a blessing in my life. I was jobless at that time because I was caregiving for my New Zealander husband who'd been bedridden for some time after he came out from the hospital. I had no money of my own, and my husband's pension at that time was not even enough for all the medicines that he was taking; he was also on oxygen. I was aware of the financial difficulty of my son too. He was very young and very hardworking, but his salary of ten thousand pesos per month was not enough for his family. He had three children, two of whom were twin babies, he was renting his house for three thousand five hundred a month, plus the water and electric bills. I was worried at that time for my son, especially when his wife at that time would tell me that they were hungry and the babies had no milk. While at home taking care of my sick husband I suddenly felt the urgency of the situation to have money at that time so I picked up a pen and a notebook and wrote down "I, Jenny, now have fifty thousand pesos in my possession. You, Jenny, now have fifty thousand pesos in your possession," and so forth. Late that morning, my daughter-in-law at the time, Liezl, came by with the two hungry crying babies plus the eldest who was six years old. They looked hungry and Liezl told me that she could not produce milk anymore from her breast for the two babies, and she had no money to buy milk. The two babies were crying simultaneously and nonstop for so long, and I felt my heart sinking for them. My sick husband who was on his bed couldn't tolerate the noise, so he screamed and asked why we couldn't stop the babies from crying. I answered that they were hungry and there was no money to buy milk. On this, he gave me money enough to buy a small can of milk. Without my knowledge, Liezl silently picked up that piece of paper where I wrote the affirmations. After reading it, she told me that she knew I had fifty thousand pesos and why wouldn't I give her some money so that her problems would be solved. My affirmations were written in the present tense so that when you read it you would really believe that the money was right in my possession. I told Liezl that I had that money, but that she had to be patient and wait for me to give some of it to her anytime. She was a bit confused, but she left after I had handed her the can of milk for the babies.

That evening, I had another visitor, Lilia. She was my buddy in the Rotary Club when I was still teaching. I had not seen Lilia for two years; she just dropped by without prior notice. She said that she had been in the United States for two years on vacation with her only son, a doctor.

Lilia belongs to a well-off real estate family who owned subdivisions and apartments for rent in the city. She said she dropped by to invite me to a Chinese New Year celebration held at the casino just across the road. I didn't even know there was a casino there, or what a casino was. I had no idea; I had never been to one before. She said she remembered that I was just living nearby because she had visited me before. While in the casino I became bored. My heart was still heavy, thinking of the financial difficulty of my son and the cries of the hungry babies. When Lilia noticed my boredom she dragged me to another area. It was very noisy and she gave me two tubes of tokens. I did not understand what they were, then she found a machine and told me to sit on the chair in front of it. She then instructed me to drop three coins at a time then pull the lever each time. She left me after saying she would be back for me. It took me three drops of three coins when all of a sudden the machine went wild. I was scared. I thought I had destroyed it. I won one hundred fifty thousand pesos, the jackpot prize at that time! My fifty thousand pesos affirmation multiplied three times! Coincidence? I don't think so. I've had so many experiences similar to that, and I believe in affirmations to work in perfect timing; the perfect timing may take a long time or in an instant.

Going back to Liezl's predicament, that same night I went to my son's house and gave Leizl ten thousand pesos to solve her financial problem, and we both bought food for the family. Aside from the cash I gave to solve her overdue rent and bills, I gave her more cash for other needs, and I bought lots of groceries for the family. I never had money problems of my own. I was always provided for despite all the difficulties of my loved ones surrounding me, so I started teaching them to go to the Source of all abundance so that they themselves can draw the blessings that are intended for them. Manifestation is a process. Once your psyche is convinced of your sincerity, an opportunity suddenly appears, even knocks on your door. All you have to do is to open the door and acknowledge it. I have had some students who would complain that they had been doing the affirmation for so long and yet there was no result. As a process for manifestation, writing affirmations has the following phases:

1. Write the affirmation in the correct format.
2. Write the affirmation in the spirit of fun.
3. Write each set of three person affirmations 20 times a day for 28 days.
4. After 28 days, forget about it and just continue with your daily routine.

There will be some changes in your life in some, if not all, areas, directly or indirectly related to the affirmation you have written. If your affirmation is a difficult one or is too impossible for you to believe, there will be changes in your life like you moving from one place to another or losing your job and finding a replacement. The psyche is clearing the way. Sometimes you will lose something you thought you valued because they will be hindrances for the manifestation of what you affirmed. You have to be prepared for the changes. That's why you have to be careful in what you wish for, especially when you make an affirmation for it. All I can say is, manifestation is sure to happen when you affirm something that is important to you, sooner or later. Trust me in this. Are you now ready to make affirmations for manifestations?

Manifestation Process: My Story

February 19, 2017

WHAT WOULD YOU FEEL IF one of your most important dreams came true? You'd probably feel blessed, blissful, or lucky. What if all of your dreams or anything that you wished for and desired came to material reality? You would really feel very lucky in life, for life, and would enjoy every moment that you have, whether you are alone or with many people. You would feel rich, beautiful, lovable, lucky, and would say life is wonderful. Once you learn and know that you can easily manifest everything that you desire or that you can easily make all your dreams come true, you would never stop creating dreams or goals because you know they would all come true. But it is sad to know that there are so many quotes and messages that are spread on the net that say, to the effect: "All you want in life cannot happen to you or cannot be yours," "You have to accept and be contented with your bitter lot in life," and so on. Amazingly, most people accept these as true, and they believe in all these limiting concepts. To have expertise in manifestation and manifesting all you want is a special talent and a blessing, but could you believe that you too can acquire such ability? You cannot even believe that such talent exists, especially when you have been through a lot of frustrations and disappointments in life. The ability to manifest what you truly desire for yourself can be developed, but first you have to believe and be deeply convinced that this talent is inherent in every person alive, including you. "Necessity is the mother of invention." This statement proves right to me. I have noticed that whenever I had a need or when I was in difficult times, my mind wandered and would think on how I could get out of the situation, until I discovered that something within me could do the seemingly impossible things for me to set me free.

I discovered the fact that problems resolve themselves, life supports itself, and that this too will pass, meaning even the most difficult and overwhelming situations in our lives will not stay long because we have the definite ability to banish them away. I also learned from experience that our core beliefs and principles in life are the controlling factors that govern our situations at all times. Below is one of the many experiences I had that strengthened my faith in life.

It was one of the most difficult times of my life; the year was 2005. My son and I had a huge falling out for some reason. After our argument, he decided to leave me and my daughter, and he moved his family to another apartment. At that time, my son had just started a good job with an equally good salary that could support all his family needs. My daughter had just graduated college and was still in the process of searching for a job. My daughter and I were broke, we had no idea where to get food, and worse where to get money to pay the rent and the bills. We had become dependent on my son and now that he left us, we were also left in limbo.

But my faith was bigger than our situation. I took a pen and a notebook and wrote down these affirmations: "I, Jenny, now have a good job that I love doing by which I am well-compensated." I wrote this in the first, second, and third person twenty times. While I was writing, my daughter was washing her clothes downstairs preparing to look for a job that week; it was a Monday. Before going down to start washing her clothes, she assured me that I didn't have to work because I was already old—I was fifty at that time—and further said that it was her turn to take responsibility of the household and to take care of me. She added further that she could afford to support me once she got a job and that it would be easier for her to get a job because she was young and had a degree. In the Philippines, there is a rampant age discrimination in finding a job. My daughter is truly God's precious gift to my life. She is always sweet, good-natured and has a kind heart.

I was still writing my affirmation when my daughter's mobile rang. She ran up the stairs to the second floor of the apartment where she left her mobile. The pastor of the church, Pastor Calalang, called her and asked her if she was interested in teaching English to Korean high school students and if she could start working that same day in the afternoon. The salary was to be five thousand pesos a month, and she would only teach four hours a day. For a fresh graduate it was a good deal, as far as my daughter was concerned. She was so excited to break the news to me, and I was equally excited. But when I asked if five thousand pesos could support our needs and the bills, reminding her that the rent alone was three thousand pesos. She assured me that she would find a second job by tutoring other Korean students. I believed my daughter. She had a very good reputation to the Koreans. They liked her and many would call her and ask her to do tutorial jobs for them. My daughter was very hardworking. She had started a tutorial job, even before she graduated a degree, and her good reputation started from there.

That afternoon, my daughter started working and at five o'clock her job was done and she came home with more good news. She said that the Korean director asked her to help him find a Filipino teacher who was experienced in teaching, has a master's degree in teaching English (TESL), and who was also a licensed teacher. Meaning he had passed the PBET (Philippine Board Examination for Teachers). Immediately, my daughter replied, "That's my mom. She has a master's degree in (TESL), and she is a licensed teacher having passed the (PBET) with ten years experience in teaching high school and college." To shorten the story, the next day it was not just my daughter who went to work in the same school. The bonus is, I was given ten thousand pesos monthly salary, hence doubling my daughter's for teaching just two hours a day; I was teaching college.

The financial difficulty that my daughter and I were supposed to face in the immediate future didn't happen. We didn't even have to look for a job. We attracted the job because we established a reputation, and I will still attribute this incident to my affirmations.

Coincidence? Not so, lots of people with our qualifications would spend weeks, even months, and lots of rejections before they get a job. My psyche presented the opportunity that knocked on our door, but this time it rang the phone to present itself to us.

I reiterate the benefits we obtained, which I discussed in my previous article about writing affirmations to make them into a habit. The psyche will learn to instantaneously respond to your needs when it arises because it has stocks of wisdom in your mind's "cabinet."

A Blueprint for Your Life

February 19, 2017

WHEN I WAS SIXTEEN YEARS old and working as a colporteur missionary in IMS (International Missionary Society), I came across this statement from one of my readings: "Plan your work and work your plan." This statement became my principle in everything I have done since then. Years later when I studied for my MBA, I learned more thoroughly the importance of planning when you have certain projects you want to succeed.

Planning is the first step to success, for how can you succeed in something that never even had a goal in the first place? So in terms of your life, do you have plans? A plan is good, but to succeed is to be thorough in working out for such plan to reach its goals. A comprehensive plan should include all the details from goal setting to strategies and implementations that should be followed through or monitored to see that you are on the right track.

Your plan should follow the blueprint that you have created for yourself and your life. A blueprint is actually the framework where you should fill in the plans when needs arise, and your plan should be based on every detail. Here I draw a symbolic framework that I can see every day to remind me that I will only do things that are within this framework. This symbolic framework is for me, but anybody can be creative and make their own. What is important is to understand all the symbols and know they are meaningful to you.

The following are eight symbolic components of a complete framework that I made for the kind of life I intend to create for myself within a given period of time. I made a drawing that symbolizes these eight components of my life's framework. This drawing is shown here as an example.

1. Abundance... Abundance is symbolized here by the branch of a tree that is full of fruits and a basket. The basket represents labor or work to harvest naturally its fruit. Natural abundance is represented by the tree, which is directly connected to the ground, the "mother" earth.

2. Love... Love is represented by the symbol yin and yang. This shows that the love relationship can only be fulfilling and successful when there is perfect reciprocity.

3. Peace... Peace here is represented by a dove with young fresh leaves.

4. Beauty... There are seven stars with colors different from one another, and they are shown as coming from far away to the present. Significant to this is the sexy body of a woman, which for me would mean my sexuality and being sensuous; these are necessary feminine characteristics when used in a natural sense as represented by the flowers, the landscape, the sky, and water. Sexuality should be naturally productive and must be in its proper perspective rather than abused to insinuate others.

5. Health... Health symbol here is the restoration to the natural flow from within and outward.

6. Success... Success is represented by a bird of paradise that has finally reached the sun, the source of energy and the peak of one's potentials.

7. Happiness... Happiness is represented by a woman who is capable of leaping over obstacles. She is backed up by the source of energy, the sun.

8. Faith... Faith is the eyes that can see beyond what the immediate environment is presenting; it's wisdom.

The Magic of Writing an Ideal Scene

February 20, 2017

LIKE WRITING AFFIRMATIONS, WRITING AN ideal scene has a magical effect once your psyche becomes convinced and amenable to it. An ideal scene is a picture in your mind, a scenario where you can see clearly your new life once your dream comes true. You can write and describe the details of that scene or you can collect pictures of yourself and put it in the center of a poster where all the pictures surrounding it are the ones you have dreamed of.

In 2013, I wrote my ideal scene as follows. This one concerns my husband and me living together in America. At that time, I became hopeless about getting a visa for coming to America because of so many discrepancies in my documents. I had been denied three times by the American embassy, and I was losing hope. I was even thinking of just breaking the marriage with my husband if he would not be the one to come and live with me in the Philippines. It would have been easier for him to live in the Philippines than for me to live in America. But my husband was also more logical. His salary in America was about ten times bigger than what I was earning as a college instructor in the Philippines. Out of hopelessness, I decided to write an ideal scene, both written and in collage form. My objective in the ideal scene was for me to live in America with my husband. Here's an example on how to write an ideal scene.

First you write the title in the present tense such as this: " I am now living happily with my husband in America." Second, after writing the title in the present tense, write "Ideal Scene." Third, write the details like this: "All the discrepancies in my documents are now resolved. I have now received my US visa. I am now living with my husband in Marion, Indiana, USA. We are now enjoying the consummation of our relationship as husband and wife. My husband is very nurturing and supportive to me and vice versa." Fourth, affirm this: "This or something better now manifest for me easily and effortlessly in very satisfactory and harmonious ways for the highest good of all concerned."

In 2016, I had finally arrived here in the United States and as I saw in my ideal scene. Everything has worked perfectly in my marriage now. Once your psyche becomes amenable to your method of manifesting, whatever method you use and whatever you wish in any area of your life, the universe will dance and bow to your wishes. There is power within us that just awaits acknowledgment and exercise to make it work for us.

Living a Perfect Life

February 21, 2017

What Is a Perfect Life?

Is there such thing as a perfect life? Every person has a perfect life unique to him or her. What may be perfect for me may not necessarily be perfect for anyone else. Whether you agree or disagree is not important. Opinions have no place in a universe where everything in this whole ecosystem is predestined by the universal Law of Cause and Effect and more universal and natural laws. Just like the Law of Gravity where, as an example, when you throw anything up it will surely come back down. Such is one example of the millions of universal laws that govern all lives in general. Life can only be perfectly fulfilling when one lives the perfect life that is unique to him. But it's sad to say that per survey in all areas of life, 99.99 percent of the whole world's population is incapable of seeing, much less experiencing, the perfect life that is intended for each uniquely on the individual level. Given the preceding statement, it sounds like nobody needs a perfect life. People define and study comprehensively success, happiness, and the like whether scientifically, theoretically, philosophically, by "trial and error" but for what? Is it just to know and philosophize or theorize? Why not just live your own perfect life?

So what then is a perfect life? The answer is for you to discover. The only rule is: live the life that is unique to you. Well, find it first. Start from within yourself; it's just there. Believe it or not, it's your choice.

Life Is Like a Flower

Life is like a flower; it blossoms as the sun rises, but it withers at the end of the day. Needless to say, each of us is in this life for a predestined span of time. No one knows exactly when he is going back to the "Creator" to Mother Earth or to the unknown, but all of us know that the day comes as surely as the sun rises in the morning and hides at the end of the day. Given this premise, we can see that to have this individual life is a privilege or a gift rather than a right. What are you doing with your life? This gift? This privilege? Do you take care and develop it into its natural perfection? Or do you mess everything up so that you live in a complicated, entangled labyrinth, hence, not really living the life intended for you? Life means living, not mere existing. Living the life is its maturity and perfection. Maturity and perfection bear excellent fruits in various areas of one's life. On the other hand, mere existing is stupidly following what is right in front of you and what pleases the senses in a momentary basis. It's also trying to pleasure yourself in a temporal, messy, and entangled life. Politicians, professionals, authorities, church people, beggars, and all sorts of people are sadly in this state of entanglement.

My Perfect Life

I live my perfect life with the following strategies: 1) I know my potentials. Just discovering my potentials is by itself an endless lifelong effort; 2) I establish my potentials as the foundation and basis for creating a framework that I religiously fill in toward the achievement of any goals that I have created; 3) I develop my intuition, respect it, trust it, and then follow it sincerely in any given time and situation of my life; 4) I keep my eyes open for opportunities that fit my potentials, desires, and dreams. I create opportunities if I don't find it in my present environment; 5) I check my desires, goals, dreams, plans, strategies, and the like. I evaluate their validity, sincerity, and quality as to whether they are destructive or creative and productive, negative or positive, and so forth; and 6) I trust myself fully, and no amount of suggestions from anyone can defy the dictates of my intuition. I cannot be persuaded to do anything that detracts from my life's perfect direction, and I kick out any foolishness and entanglements that will lead to a problematic life.

To elaborate each of these principles would mean writing volumes of books. Living my perfect life is living consciously in a moment-by-moment basis and foreseeing those elements in life that don't belong to me. I know what I want for myself, and I surely get it exactly as I want, in fact better. The only rule is, I only live the life that is intended for me according to my natural potentials. Everybody is born complete with potentials to live his unique perfect life. Yet, almost everybody dies a perfect Xerox copy of all the miseries and entanglements of one another in a given environment and culture.

It Only Takes a Spark to Keep the Fire Going

February 22, 2017

IT ONLY TAKES A SPARK to keep the fire going. It was all too good to be true, and whatever is too good to be true is oftentimes backed up with some creeping fears of "what ifs." What if this situation that I am enjoying won't last? What if he changes? What if I am just living in a dream and suddenly I wake up and ooops!

The house we rented was beautiful and new. It had three bedrooms, three bathrooms, and a spacious master bedroom with a beautiful and spacious jacuzzi inside it. At the back of the house was a beautiful cottage for the servants. We had a stay-in housemaid named Lourdes who did all the chores for us in this wonderful house. My fourteen-year-old daughter, Jean, my late husband, Adrian, and me were the only occupants in this house. The neighborhood was perfect. Across the road was the Korean Mr. Kho. At the right over the fence was the American Mr. Fisher, and on the left side was the Filipino engineer Ratunel. My New Zealander (Kiwi) husband, Adrian Shiels, was co-owner of three hotels. There were sixteen Australians and New Zealand citizens who pooled together their resources to form a corporation, and then ran the hotel business in Balibago, Angeles City, and the Philippines. They ran three hotels there. I used to work as the bookkeeper, and at the same time the manager for the Filipino employees in one of the hotels. But then there were lots of things, activities, and situations in the business that were contradictory to my value system. So one day I decided to leave the job. I decided to "burn bridges."

In my core belief system was the conviction that I was a born teacher or a public speaker or lecturer. The job situation in the hotel had nothing to do with my accepted natural inclinations. I liked the money and the comforts of life all right, but what about me? What about the "real me"? What about the "born teacher" who was screaming deep inside me? I had been a teacher since time immemorial. Even when I was barely nine years old, I was already a Sabbath school teacher every Saturday for children's department in the church. It went on and on, even when I was a missionary/colporteur in the International Missionary Society.

To be working in a hotel, especially patronized by sex tourists in our country, was a great insult and challenge to my core value system. I had realized that money and comfort in living was not all there was to satisfy the longings of the soul. Deep within me was a vacuum that demanded fulfillment. I cannot ignore me, I cannot ignore the "self," who I call Senotiza, who screams for justice in her existence to this world. She always reminded me of who I really was and that I didn't belong in that job. The prostitutes, the sex tourists, the vicious and lascivious clients who filled the hotel premises were not the types of people I could tolerate in my everyday life. I remember the honor and dignity of the job that I had been in for years and years. Honor and dignity versus comfort in living and money without dignity is just rubbish for "Senotiza." There has to be a balance; honor+ dignity=money+comfortable life=fulfillment

It only takes a spark for us to be reminded of who we really are, and then we burn bridges to separate us from everything that is not our personal reality. And once the fire starts burning we will be back to our original state of existence—the most fulfilling and perfect life that each of us can choose to live.

Life as it Is

February 23, 2017

Happiness is...

With my loved ones
What is the meaning of life?
A time for everything...

Songs of Solomon 3:1 has this to say: "There is an appointed time for everything. And there is a time for every event under heaven." When I was about five years old, my dad left me and my three-year-old little sister Lily in the house of my auntie Tutay. She was older than my dad, and she was a language teacher who taught Spanish in college. During one of our dinnertimes, this was one of those very significant events in my life that left a mark on my belief system. There was lots of food on that long table. Our nine much older cousins, whose ages ranged from twelve to thirty-two, also surrounded that long table full of a variety of food. My sister and I were the "babies" and felt so tiny and insignificant in their midst, but they were very accommodating, loving, and caring to us. My auntie was a very jolly and energetic old lady and would always raise some thought-provoking questions. My sister and I only had one fried egg for each as compared to their crabs, roasted pork, fish, and all the other food; they got that. This happened for all the dinners that we were there. I can see how they enjoyed all the food on the table. No, it was not because they were selfish and did not share their food with my sister and me; it was because of my dad's religion, which was different from my auntie's, in which my daad warned my auntie never to feed us with "flesh food" while he was away. My auntie knew what would happen if she disobeyed my dad; he was the brother with the worst tantrum in the family.

While everybody was eating, in which my twenty-six-year-old-nurse cousin Benita, noticed me watching them eat sumptuously, she asked me, "Jenny, aren't you envious of us eating all these delicious food while you and Lily only have that fried egg?" That question actually made me think. I was five years old, but everybody would attest that I behaved like a matured person in my speech. They labeled me "little wonder girl" because of my questions that needed sincere and serious answers, especially from adults. My answer to Cousin Benita's question was, "Papa said that if we eat fish and meat, especially pork, God will burn us in hell." This answer caused some sort of provocation to all my cousins around, but they were all considerate. But then Cousin Benita had this to say, "Our God is very kind and loving. He would never burn us in hell no matter what we eat, for as long as the food is good and we enjoy them." This answer, and a lot more probing on this subject between me and my cousins, convinced me of their sensible contentions. From then on, I started eating meat and would always question my dad for any rules he imposed on us children, on me specifically. But since I was just a child, my dad always won, at least for the time being. In my adult life, my dad found me very difficult to control because I had learned to live independently and choose what to believe and live my life according to my own convictions. It all started from that dinner conversation when I was five.

Living my life now
Just living my life
I had lived my childhood;
I had lived my teen years;
I had lived my youth;
I lived them in my every moment;
Nobody lived my life for me;
But I learned from every person who came along;
Each of them doesn't need to be agreeable at all times;
But certainly, each had taught me a lesson or more;
That contributed to my being me in my here and now;
And even in my years to come.

Life Is but a Dream: Yesterday, Today, and Tomorrow

February 24, 2017

YESTERDAY WAS LIVED. WE WERE all there with the tiny shoes that we cannot wear anymore; with the mother whose home is not our home anymore; with the teacher we love or fear; and with all the deeds, the fashion and style, the places, the people, and the things or objects we used to possess and enjoy. We just leave them behind with the passing of time, with growth and mobility that life demands from us or expects from us. Yesterday was lived and I have no regrets.

Today I count my blessings and thank the Great Intelligence for the life I enjoy today. Today is the fulfillment of the dream I dreamed yesterday. And because I am alive, I continue to dream. My dream for tomorrow will be my today as time passes by; hence, in my dream, I create my "today" for the kind of life I will have in my tomorrow.

Tomorrow will be my today. How I dream and what dreams I have today will be my life in my tomorrow.

Life is but a dream. Without the dream, life has no direction and there is nothing to hope for. Without the dream, life is not life at all; it's just mere existence. There will not be a today in our tomorrow, and we don't even have a "today." Did you live yesterday? If yes, then you live your "today." Yesterday is but a dream gone, and today is a dream-creation for the kind of tomorrow that we dream of.

Introspection: Self-Appreciation

February 25, 2017

SELF-APPRECIATION IS DIFFERENT FROM EGOTISM. Appreciating ourselves and our lives is praising and thanking God for creating us and giving value to what God has done in our lives; whereas egotism, on the other hand, is comparing yourself to others and becoming proud for the feelings and thoughts that you are better than them. Self-appreciation is simply acknowledging your value as a person, giving value to the reason that God has created you as a person and what you are going to do with your life. The following is my self-appreciation in an introspective form:

Nobody else can love me the way I do to myself.

Nobody else is with me in every second of my life.

I am the only living thing who is with me all the way since birth to present.

No one else knows me from inside out but me.

I am the only person who can know my feelings and my thoughts in any moment of my life.

I was there at every turn of my life and in every event, people, object, and place that occurred in every phase of my life. People come and go and so with relationships.

Money and all the material things I love that come with it all pass by.

Jobs and careers come and go.

Places I'd been have been left behind so I can move to one that suits me and my needs in a given time, but in all these, I am still with me and I am the one who knows and experiences all the thoughts and the feelings involved in every occurrence, in every step, and in every phase of my life. I know myself better than anyone else could know about me; therefore, I am the only person who can love me and accept me completely as I am.

Nobody eats the food for me when I am hungry.

Nobody studied the lessons for me so I could pass my exams when I was a student, and so on.

Nobody felt the grief for me when my husband died. Nobody cried for me for my loss and even if they did, I still grieved and cried for myself.

My parents loved me completely, but they loved me because I was their child and they had dreams for me, which I probably could not dream for myself. Sometimes they were around, but not every time I needed them.

My husband loves me because I am his wife who he may be happy and proud about and whose company he can enjoy for his certain needs, but I cannot know exactly what is in his mind and in his heart, and vice versa.

I have flaws, I make many mistakes, I made wrong decisions, and I fail on many of my dreams and aspirations. Even loved ones criticize me and point their fingers at me. Friends and lovers may prove untrue, all the unfairness in life may happen, and no one may stand by me, but I have my Self, my reliable Self who forgives all my mistakes and flaws and who is sincerely compassionate of my weaknesses.

The Self that assures me that everything passes by and that every moment is a moment of revival and of coming back to the "Self" who truly knows me.

I am the one who knows why things happen the way they do in my life, and so I can always change course when things go wrong.

No one else can make major decisions for me when it comes to my life's destiny. I am my own perfect decision maker for myself because if I make wrong decisions, I am the one who suffers most. I love myself.

I know that I am a wonderful creature and I am capable of handling my own life to make it better and better in all aspects. Whatever other people say against me does not bother me because I know who I am.

People may judge me according to their measure, but I accept myself completely as I am and I allow myself to explore life according to the guidance of the "still small voice" that speaks to me at every turn of the way.

I trust that voice inside me; it is the one who has been with me all the way. It is excellently reliable; I see my own truth and reality and I like it.

I love everything that I am, that I do, and that I possess.

I love myself completely as I am, including my pains, my flaws, my mistakes, my failures, my hardships, my difficulties, my struggles, and my endeavors.

I trust myself completely and I never betray "me."

No one else can understand and accept me completely as I do myself.

I have no other life; this is me and I cherish myself.

I cherish my precious life so I don't allow anyone to affect me.

If I am not 100 percent for "me" through and through, will anyone be for me all the way?

No, they have their own self to attend to.

The Process of Socialization

February 26, 2017

MAN IS A SOCIAL BEING, and as the saying goes: "No man is an island." Human beings cannot stand alone without other humans to mold them and fit them into a certain society and the world as a whole. What you are at present is the by-product of who you have been in the past, and your genes, your perception, and interaction with the whole ecosystem that raised you from birth to present. Each personality is an accumulation of the complex cultural influences and his natural and inherent tendencies in any given condition and phase of development. No one has the right to judge anyone else because we are all different from one another both inherently and socially. Matthew chapter 7 in the Bible says something very significant about judging others: "Judge not so you won't be judged; for whatever mete you measured to others will be measured back to you." We all differ on who and what type of people we mingled with in our development, and these people have a very strong impact and influence in the way we behave and in our decision-making activities. This is also the reason for the adage: "Tell me who your companions are and I will tell you who you are." Personally, I made some introspection on who I had been with in the past, and I grouped them into the following:

1. Parents, siblings, children, husband/s, and other "heart relationships" (family and loved ones)

2. Servants and employees

3. Peer groups

4. Clients

5. Sales people

6. Employers and big bosses

7. Students

8. Social groups

9. The public

There could be more, but these are the major people who are found on my horizon; I could write volumes of books if I wrote for each of them.

The adage: "Tell me who your companions are and I will tell you who you are" is a perfect statement to measure the type of personality we have become. Are you sociable? Shy? Introvert? Extrovert? Ambivert? Candid? Secretive?

Whether we agree or not or whether we are aware of it or not, each of us is a by-product of both our inherent and hereditary qualities and the socialization processes we were into. This includes the total socioeconomic-demographic and the complete cultural value system we come from and accumulated over the years. The English anthropologist Edward Tylor defined culture as "a complex whole which includes knowledge, belief, art, law, morals, customs and any other capabilities acquired by people as members of a society." These are just few of what a person deems important in the core of his personality and are demonstrated in his behavior, decision making, and lifestyle. We are mainly what we are now on the personality level and in our socialization and interpersonal relationships because of what we have been through culturally and what kind of people we have been socializing with, and these are in addition to our inherent qualities.

Whether I like it or not and whether I am aware or not, each group of people have great impact of who I am now.

Family and Loved Ones

I am the firstborn, not to mention that I was born at the time when my mom and dad had lost their hope of ever having children after twenty-one years of marriage. So it is normal that I got all the attention, love, and adoration from my parents and the two siblings that followed me. I had to be good. My parents had high expectations from me because I should be the role model for my two younger siblings. They both looked up to me in all of their endeavors in life. And my family was small. This family setting and my place in the family had a big impact on my character and personality. I tend to become an achiever and feel loved and worthy of admiration. I carried out this character and personality even in choosing and handling my love life relationships in my later years. I had an inherent attitude of "If you love me, you're lucky. You have to be faithful to me because if you hurt my feelings, I will instantly kick you out from my life. That's easy for me to do because I don't need you. I am the one needed; I am not in need."

Servants and Employees (the household servant or what we locally called the "maid")

I always had a maid since time immemorial. In my childhood, both my parents were busy in their respective businesses and preoccupations during the day so we had all types of servants to run the household and to babysit us when we were kids. Whether throughout my marriage life or when I was living alone, I always had at least one maid to do the chores. Hence, having a maid is not a luxury for me; it's a necessity because my mind and time is always busy with something else. If I were to count how many maids have come my way, I would say it wouldn't be less than a hundred. So, I have a fairly good comparison of the types of personalities of these people. I should be more understanding even with their false pride and self-assessments. I am tolerant to them to a certain extent.

It would be a very long story if I had to explain each of the groups of people I had associated with in the past that contributed to who I am in my present. The bottom line is our characters, personalities, and even temperaments are molded by the types of people who surround us in a given time and place, and most of all by our socioeconomic standing in a given environment and society.

Know the types of people and their characters and value systems that surround you; they are the mirrors of your personality and the kind of life that you live.

Just a Little Glimpse of Light

February 27, 2017

THE FOLLOWING NARRATIVE POEM WAS a symbolic expression of my true feelings when life was so hard to bear. Life is wonderful, never boring. There are twists and turns and turning points that happen along the journey of development. Anyone who would say that his life is boring because there is nothing significant that has happened to him is not really living his life; he just exists. We have to acknowledge and embrace every situation. To embrace life is to feel every given situation, be it blissful or hurting. To embrace joy and happy experiences encourages repetition of that blissful moment and is actually an act or a ritual to summon more wonderful things to happen again in our lives. To embrace sad, hurting, and difficult life situations reminds us that we are fallible humans, that we make mistakes; hence, this acknowledgment will make us better persons once we get out from such situations. It also reminds us of the essence of the statement: this too will pass. Therefore, we can summon courage to get us through. It will make us bolder to face any life situation and new ventures, and when success happens it reminds us not to be boastful because nothing is permanent in this life. Here's my expression at the darkest moment of my life:

Groping in the cold and the seemingly unending darkness that
encompasses this particular night of my soul; in the cold night
when I was lost for some confusing reasons;

My heart longed for the Light, just a glimpse of light to guide me home;

To the home where merry hearts and abundance in everything good
thrive;

Where Love and praises to the beauty of this Universe and its Creator
warms every soul;

My limbs are numbed from the cold;

My heart is painfully pounding for the fear of the dark;

Such darkness where a monsters might appear to devour me into pieces;

In this darkness where no one exactly knows what evil might happen?

Who can rescue me from this horrible situation and condition?

I cannot even see; everything is just darkness and I don't know where
I am; not a step would my numbed and painful legs do;

Where is home?

Where are my parents who care for me?

Do they remember me?

Do they know that I am lost?

If so are they going to look for me and eventually find me?

It seems like eternity in this condition;

I have been crying too long and quietly, afraid to even scream,
otherwise the evil ones might be the first to hear me;

I long for home;

Just thinking of the comforts in my home give me some strength;

I just need some glimpse of light now;

I can see how important the Light is, now that I am lost in this darkness;

Then suddenly a little light is moving…just a dot of light is wonderful
to follow in a darkness like this;

As I crawled to follow the Light, I realized that it grew bigger and it
    continued to move as if guiding me;

As the Light increased its brightness, I started to see the grasses that
    surrounded me, and I remembered where this place was;

I knew where I was and I knew what direction I should be going;

This knowledge alone was enough to provide me strength to carry
    on, if it was just to crawl toward the comforts of my home.

The Magic of Turning Your Worries into Creativity

February 28, 2017

HAVE YOU EVER MET ANYONE who has never felt worries once in a while in all his life? Everybody, in one way or another and in certain degrees, have had worries in life. Even the seemingly jolly and successful person carries in his head certain worries that he often is not aware of.

The year 2008 was my third year of teaching back in SPCC main campus; I had left my post as the chair at the College of Business Administration, AWOL in 1999 when I realized how sick my late husband, Adrian Shiels, was. He needed 100 percent attention because he was on oxygen throughout the two years that he was bedridden. When Adrian died in 2003, I suffered depression and was sulking in grief in my bedroom; I didn't leave the house for a year. My friends and colleagues thought that I had left the country because I warned all my family members not to tell anyone of my whereabouts, "howabouts" and "whatabouts." Actually, I was not completely sulking; my heart and mind could not hold all those painful negative thoughts and feelings for too long. In the interim, I had bouts of depression, sadness, worry, discouragement, and I lost my desire to live. I was fifty and among my negative self-inflicting thoughts were my weakening will and the loss of desire to live anymore. My worries were of being out of a job, being broke, and at my age nobody would hire me. I had lost any source of income.

My son was married already with three small children, and my daughter was still in college as a working student in SPCC. My son's salary was not enough for all the bills and rent and all of us, seven members in the family. We were jam-packed in that small two-bedroom apartment. That was the "dark era" in my life. I could hear my daughter-in-law's whining every day, and in addition to my inner turmoils, this whining really nailed me to the wall. I just lost courage to live let alone work again.

Knowing my reality, I remembered the adage: "Necessity is the mother of invention." Necessity, yes, that was the situation in my family. There was a dire need for a change, yet I could not figure out what I could do to ease the needy condition that we all were in. Realizing the situation, I still didn't exert any outward effort to change the situation; rather, I started to remember who I was. The first thing I did was I just got my pen and notebook, my colors, my white bond paper, and started writing everything about who I really was, my skills, my profession, my education, and so forth. Then I wrote down what I deserved in life and drew them in the bond paper.

I had been doing all these introspection and self-assessments in the one year that I was sulking inside my bedroom. Then one day out of the blue, the billionaire lady, Mrs. Jojo Haynes, came to visit me. She learned about me through my daughter-in-law. I didn't know her at the time and had never heard of her let alone her socioeconomic status. She had been looking for a person who had my educational status and skills. At first I refused to accept her offer and her request for my help concerning her undergrad thesis in AB Psychology. She had already hired a PhD to do her thesis, but she failed and had wasted one year just to do it all over again. The offer was a salary equivalent to my professional fee as a chair in a college, plus such benefits as housing me in an expensive three-bedroom condominium in Manila, complete with a housemaid, a modern automatic car with its driver, free complete three meals a day, among other things. I still refused the unusually attractive offer; it was just too good to be true for me. But her persistence, six times coming back to me, finally impressed me. It was unbelievable that this rich lady was having such high regard of me and with such 100 percent trust in me and my capability, so I accepted the offer. I could not help myself asking why. Did my affirmation "I, Jenny, now have a satisfying and well-compensating job" written twenty times every day in first, second, and third person and within two months' time work? I just knew one thing. I changed my mind from worrying to creating, even in the mental and "writing" efforts only. What was truly amazing was, after working satisfactorily with Jojo—she had the top-graded thesis, er...the thesis I made for her and my coaching—I received lots of job offers, and even SPCC, where I left my post five years ago without a leave of absence or asking or telling anyone that I was leaving my post, rehired me.

So, in the third year of this come back to SPCC, Atty Robert John Donesa, the HRD at the time, was seen sitting in my office every morning when I arrived at work. I asked him why he did that when his office was located several buildings away from my office. His answer was, "I would like to know your secrets on why you are not affected with all the problems and gossips and politickings in this school." I just smiled and said, "I just know how to turn worry into creativity."

Acknowledging the Importance of Your Value System

March 1, 2017

What is a value system and how does it govern your lifestyle?

On people, sheep, and snails:

People are likened to a herd of sheep and to snails.

Sheep must herd together and must follow one another. A sheep must follow the butt of the one closest to its eyes; otherwise, it will go astray and will get lost for good. Sheep, by nature, are shortsighted. They don't have to think independently; they just follow blindly and that is all they have in all their lives.

Similar to sheep, people are social beings too. They need one another to base the direction of the individual life, to warm their hearts, to inspire mental activities and attitudes, and perhaps to put colors into their lives. These are only among the other complex reasons to need other people. There is nothing wrong if people are likened to sheep being social beings, but to base completely your lifestyle with the rest of the people surrounding you would mean that you are short of using your God-given ability to think and respect your personal desires to better yourself.

Similarly, a snail is cold so it needs another snail, or anything, to warm its body. It'll use whatever is closest to it regardless of qualification and quantification to warm its life. Like a snail, people are normally warm and molded by the nature of its belonging to a social group or environment, subculture, or the culture as a whole. But human beings are given the choice, unlike snails. People have the inherent ability to choose the kind of life and culture that could inspire them, and they should live, on the individual level.

The difference between people and these lower forms of animals is that humans are endowed with the ability to think. They can choose what to think, they can qualify and prequalify the nature of their thought processes, and they are far above in the nature of their intellectual capacity, which, when compared to brutes, can be unlimited if they choose to.

To think is to rationalize, in which one questions the validity and values of an idea or a premise. The following are some questions, if answered in the core of your being, could lead to finding within yourself what value system dominates your flow of thinking.

What do you value most in your life?

How much do you value your job?

Which is more important to you, the job you have or a certain relationship that may have conflict with such job?

In terms of a value system, I would like to quote biblical verses in Matthew 6: 25-34to the effect: "…do not worry about your life, or about your body…on what to eat, what to wear, what to drink…the body is more than food and clothing…the birds and the lilies don't worry and work but are fed and are arrayed with beauty;…people are more of value than the birds and the lilies…worrying cannot change things."

Value yourself more than anything else, and base your value system on this idea.

By nature, human beings are supposedly far higher in value than anything natural and man-made in this world. What you value most is the most important thing that could affect the quality of your life in any phase. Anyone who can see the essence of these statements can have a much better life than any of those unwanted situations. Just straighten out your value system. You can do that; you are naturally equipped with such ability. Just search it within you and once you have found it, then you will be courageous enough to discover and live the life you deserve.

Life Is Mobility Plus Variety

March 2, 2017

Among my favorite philosophical quotes is Heraclitus': "No one steps on the same river twice." I was in my MAE (Master of Arts in Education) philosophy class in 1988 when I first encountered this statement. My instant question was, why did he say this? Of course, at that time my normal way of thinking could not see the logic of this statement. I can always step on the same river a million of times if I so desired. There was no answer for me at that time; theorizing and philosophizing were shallow justifications to that statement.

I had to live years more before Heraclitus' statement recurred every now and then, in which it gradually unfolded and made sense in my mind. It still helps me understand certain situations as I live my life.

The river has a natural current that keeps flowing and pushing downward toward the direction of the ultimate body of water, the sea or the ocean. The next time you step on it, it won't be the same water you stepped on previously.

Similarly, life has several "currents" that keep it moving. But unlike the river where the flow is just downward and coming from just one direction, which is from a higher ground, "currents" in life come from various directions and can go astray, upward, downward, or sideways to nowhere in a variety of forms and degrees. Most often, if one is not aware of it, and always the case for those who understand the workings of the psyche, the strongest currents come from within the person, and these forces or currents invite allies from outside forces to strengthen and perpetuate its natural tendency.

To cite an example, among the millions of complexities and varieties of "currents" or forces that cause one's life to move is either the lack or the excess of money, along with money is what money can buy and where money comes from. Again, for a variety of reasons, money is a constant in every person's mind and life eventually. One major reason, though, is that money is a tool to make the quality of living better or worse, depending on its availability in one's life and on the degree, variety, complexity, and number, among others, of the "current" needs or desires to be met for a certain individual in a given time.

How Money Become a Current or Force That Moved My Life

My sight, my smile, eating (teeth), my breath, my health, among other parts of my body, are necessary for my existence and enjoyment in life. Without money and the source of money (people, loved ones) who care enough for me to live normally, I wouldn't have life now. I would either be literally dead or just existing.

A river or a body of water that has sidetracked from the main river because of a flood and some other reason, and has stayed in that new location, will eventually either stink, discolor, or become a habitat of deadly bacteria (therefore detrimental to the environment and its inhabitants, particularly people) for being stagnant or just drying up through evaporation in the air and the heat of the sun. It is not a river anymore but an offshoot, a dead offshoot.

I would have been blind, toothless, ugly, and famished, just existing, counting the days of a short and difficult breathing condition till my breath would completely run out, dead.

These names will live on with me: Rey, Ronald, Greg. I call them the extension of my life; their pockets are their investments, not to mention their love. Rey is my son and my sight. Ronald is a philanthropist friend and my smile. And last but not the least, Greg is my hubby and my heart and breath.

Can you follow how the river flows, ere, the direction of my thinking? From Heraclitus to my life, the current lives on or the forces live on. The formula is just an integral part, if not implied.

Ten Tips to Look Younger than Your Age

March 3, 2017

I HAVE VERY GOOD REASONS to write about this subject because of my own experience. I was fifty-five years old when my three grandchildren ages nine (the twins) and thirteen at the time went shopping at the mall in Cebu City. While shopping, my grandchildren would call me "Lola," which is how we call "grandma" in the Philippines. Some of the salesladies there were watching us, and one of them asked one of my grandchildren why they were calling me Lola. He answered, "Because she is our grandma." The salesladies laughed because they thought I was their aunt. They further said that I was too young to be a grandma. When I told them I was not young, I was fifty-five, they laughed because they thought that I was just thirty or younger. That was very flattering, but there are many incidents similar to this, and many have asked me about what secrets I have to stay younger looking.

There is no secret but aside from the genes, I do have some secrets that I believe work for me and that I am sharing here.

By the way, why do I have to discuss this seemingly mundane and vain subject? Well, the bottom line is we want to live life, not just exist, and life is good and beautiful if we are healthy and youthful, so there is some logic to this discussion.

Conceit aside, I write this article because of people who asked me how I maintain youthfulness because I don't look sixty-two. Whether they are sincere or not, I know what is true to me. It's no big deal actually whether I look younger than my age or not. What's important is I love myself and I am in love with life as a whole. People would compare me to my younger sister and would say that I look much younger than she is; they also compare me to some of my friends, who are much younger than me. They compare me to anybody younger than me, and they say that I look younger than them. In short, they don't believe that I am sixty-two; most would say that I am in my forties, even thirties at times.

The comments on my youthful look would have been flattering if I didn't know my truth. But I do have some tips on how to "look" younger than your age:

1. In your mind, see yourself as the ever youthful "Jenny" or whatever your name is. Scrutinize the young you: your hair, your skin, your clothes, your emotions, your movement, and behavior in any given situation. How old are you as you see yourself in your mind? How you see yourself will reflect on how people will see you.

2. Be aware of and assess your feelings and responses to any situation in your life, in people, in animals, in objects, in places, in any incidents…

3. Smile and laugh a lot with friends and loved ones; choose to see the brighter side of life and the beauty of nature.

4. Maintain a positive outlook in life. Don't look and feel like you are beaten; express your emotions and be charmingly cheerful.

5. Joy, peace, and happiness that emanate from within will glow in your outward expressions and countenance; have a joyful and positive mental attitude.

6. Take care of your health by eating the right foods and doing the right exercises for you; be consistent.

7. Be assertive with your beauty regimen by wearing fashionable clothes and accessories fitting your personality.

8. Be conscious in looking fresh all the time by paying attention to your skin, nails, and hair; keep them clean, healthy, and attractive.

9. Keep dreaming, live your dreams, love beauty, love the arts and music; be creative and productive by regularly doing your hobbies.

10. Most importantly, love, love, and love; most of all love and accept yourself completely as you are, and as you do with others.

Notice that six out of the ten tips come from within; what is within so is without. Our world of tangible reality is just the reflection of our personal inner world. Of course there are the inherent genes, along with environmental and cultural factors, but even with these, there is still a way to alter nature through willpower, consistence, and persistence. There you go! These are the only things I do that keep me young at heart, in thoughts and in looks. Life is full of natural beauty and fun, so in the spirit of fun I live to embrace all of life, the pain and the sorrows included. There is so much to enjoy in life that my psyche forgets the time, the aging.

Walk Home with Me; Life's Journey

March 5, 2017

THE FOLLOWING NARRATIVE POEM IS my personal journey in my relationships. Humans as social beings need company. Those who have been in romantic relationships know that life is more beautiful, colorful, and meaningful when they have someone who deeply loves and cares for them. But what happens to your life when this someone is gone from your life by any reasons? There is a saying that goes: "It's better to have loved and lost than never to have loved at all."

Another saying that catches my attention is: "There is always someone for each of us." Nothing is permanent in life. People in your life come and go, even your children grow and they go out on their own to live. Money comes and goes, and properties and possessions come and go. What remains is your life and everything that is you in a given time, body, soul, and spirit for as long as you are still alive.

Even the spouse you married and you stay married with till death is not the same person you first married. There are a lot of changes between the two of you, including the quality of your relationship, good or bad. There is always a change to both of you on the personal level.

My own experience in terms of relationship is when my partner died or when we experienced separation due to personal incompatibility. The longest time that I spent with no one to love me was two years, and then another one came along to offer me company. I personally know of many women who don't desire to have a partner in life anymore after the hurting breakup they experienced in their previous relationship, or for other reasons that they alone can see. Some of them have secret longings to experience love again, but they just cannot find the person they think would match their personality or who meets their standards for a desired partner in life.

For these women, I would suggest get deep within yourself and discover what you really want. If there is hatred within your heart or some phobia for having another person in your life, face it by affirming, "I love myself completely as I am including all my flaws. I am a loving and lovable person. My perfect mate comes to me easily and effortlessly." If you do this consistently, somebody will again knock on your door and offer love and companionship to you.

Here's the poem:

I walk along the highway of a lifetime journey;
I started with both my parents and siblings walking side by side with me;
Together we walked on life's wide road, with spirits high in hope,
    faith, love, and security.
For whatever reasons, I suddenly found myself walking alone;
My parents and siblings went their own ways, to each his own;
I wanted to turn back and trail them, but I was confused about
    whose road to follow;
For each was trailing a road apart from one another.
I screamed to them to wait for me;
Or for them to follow the road I took, but they obviously never
    heard me;
Instead I heard a voice that said,

"Follow your own path and stick to it." And when I tried once more
to look their way,

Before my eyes they just faded away.

I am so lonely and afraid now that I am all alone on this wide and
dusty road;

I know not what to do; I just know that I have to move on;

Hoping that somewhere along the way our paths will meet and we
will be together once more.

And so I walk on with a heavy heart;

When I notice that someone else is walking beside me;

He holds my hands as he says, "Fear not; I am with you."

In my confusion I welcome him, for is it not that in this journey, two
is better than one?

I need his company, or any good company in this journey.

He seems to be attentive to my needs;

He provides me food when I am hungry and water to quench my thirst;

He shields me from the cold and from the rain and even from the
biting heat of the sun;

He helps me to take another step onward when my legs are tired and
weary;

And carry me with his strong arms when I cannot make it on my own;

For all the good things that he does to me;

How can I be convinced that he is my perfect mate throughout this
endless journey?

We continue to walk together as we move on this life's pathway;

This time I carry our daughter while he holds our son who walks
beside him;

My joy and confidence cannot be contained for having a family of
my own walking with me;

The stranger that used to be is now the loving father of my children.

But then life's journey has twists and turns;

Sometimes the road splits in two or more;

And when I turn to look, I find out that one is missing along the way.

We are walking with my two siblings on this journey for decades more;

Now I realize that it's just my grown-up children and me walking on this journey;

And now I walk on with my children by my side, with hearts full of hope for the bright home ahead;

But once again, on life's highway, there are always crossroads and twists and turns;

Until I find once again that my company is another stranger;

The stranger who finally walks home with me.

Life Is a Series of Individual Choices

March 4, 2017

A happy outlook and a positive disposition in life brings blessings and attracts good luck.

Love Lifted Me

When difficult times seem to hover on the horizon of our lives, my Mommy used to sing this: "I was sinking deep in sin (oblivion and confusing situations) far from the peaceful shore; Buried deeply stained within, sinking to rise no more; But the Master of the sea heard my despairing cry; From the waters lifted me now safe am I. Love lifted me..."

In any given situation, where gloomy conditions appear—when we have done our best but what we aspire still fails—we have two choices: choose to despair and accept ourselves as losers or choose to know and affirm our true value as dignified human beings. "When nothing else could help, Love lifted me..." was another song that inspired me ever since my childhood to this day. When everything else fails and nothing else can help, all I do is to remember who I am. Remembering who I truly am—and counting my blessings and affirming my true state of being and the wholesome experiences with God and the universe—have actually made my life flow easily, even a midst life's "tempestuous waves."

Such collective experiences during family devotional hours impressed in me a positive outlook in life, which became the strong foundation that our parents instilled in us siblings.

A Family That Prays Together Stays Together

Some people tend to despise those who adhere to some religious practices in the family. They seem to forget that, as the smallest social unit, the strength of a family relationship goes a long, long way throughout life's twists and turns. They would brand religiously inclined people or their siblings as being brainwashed. A strong family foundation generally makes a person strong. Family religious practices such as praying together during the devotional hour and going to church together are blessings if done in the spirit of family fun. Being together or in unity and family camaraderie, rather than being imposed by the parents as the only way to get to heaven, must be the essence of religious practices in the family. Fanaticism should be deliberately discarded.

The Effects of My Religious Background on My Outlook in Life

My siblings and I developed strong self-values and high self-esteems because of the strong foundation we experienced during our childhood. In the process of personal growth and development, I discovered a pattern for myself, which I lived by. I can sense when things are not going right so that I can take charge of my life and choose what path to follow. When things really go wrong to the extent that I sometimes feel like everything seems to be out of my control, then I pray and meditate; this is my refuge, the source of my strength. Prayer and meditations are habits; hence, they would have started early on in life. This wholesome and powerful habit normally originates from family practices. Lots of people talk about meditating, but they just cannot do it consistently; they need to develop the habit. Any person who try to analyze me according to their shallow and acquired way of thinking, may say anything, negative or positive, that they perceive about me but nothing can affect me whatsoever because I know exactly who I am, and I know that only me and my God can know who I am. No one else can know me and everything there is to know about me, better than I do; hence, no one and nothing can run me down or let me down except when I allow it to happen. Remembering who I am and my "power" within that emanates from the Source of all Intelligence, which I had learned from an early age to be working for me, fades away or banishes any negative influences from the wickedness of any human. I am protected by the Divine Guidance and Providence.

My Affirmations About Myself, a Positive Outlook, a Daily Meditation...

This is me; this is my life. No one else can live my life for me in every second of it. I appreciate everything that I am, everything I do, and everything that I acquire and possess. I have a reliable power within me that works for me at every turn. This power within me is my inherent gift from the Origin of all Powers and Great Intelligence that governs natural laws. When in difficulty and when nothing else can help, this power within me lifts me up and raises me to a higher ground. If I fail in one area of my life, then I can turn and choose to focus on those areas I am good at. The deeper I sink into oblivion, the higher I rebound. Remembering this principle and pattern of my life brings me back to my true state of being.

These or something better now manifests for me easily and effortlessly in very satisfactory and harmonious ways for the highest good of all concerned.

Motherhood Is a Lifetime Job

March 6, 2017

I AM A MOTHER, NOT to mention being a grandmother of seven wonderful grandchildren, for now. Becoming a mother for the first time was a life-changing experience. It was one of, if not *the*, most wonderful experiences for a woman. This wonderful experience—if you do your duty and responsibility with the inherent love of a mother—is the kind of love that is as great as God's love to all humanity, the kind of love that is unconditional and is willing to lay down one's life for the good of the loved ones. I am writing this article because I see the importance of a mother's role in molding her children to become assets of society instead of having her children be liabilities. It would be a mother's nightmare if one of her children became a criminal or lived his/her life waywardly. A mother's love begins even before she has children, even before she becomes pregnant, even before she falls in love with any man. She already has that kind of motherly longings and instinct to reproduce another human that could be the object of her love. This should be one of the many wonders of being a woman. If this is so, the world should have been filled with productive and successful human beings. I will begin my story long before I became a mother myself. That was the time I realized that I was mother material, someone who could produce wonderful, beautiful, and successful children of my own.

On Becoming a Mother's Heart

Like any normal mother, I love my son and would shake the whole universe if necessary just so my son could have a good life. I am not a typical mother though, so I cannot expect my firstborn to be a typical son either. It all started when I happened to become so attracted to this very beautiful six-month-old baby boy.

I was nineteen years old then when I went to my classmate's house to get the book she borrowed from me. I saw the baby there; he was my classmate's nephew. The baby's name was Roland and what attracted me to him was his very healthy features, his flawless and glowing baby skin, the giggles, and everything a wonderful baby could be. I stayed almost a day there just watching and playing with Roland. That was the first time I had spent so much time with a baby. This experience of attraction to a baby haunted me from then on. In my fantasy, I imagined myself having a baby like that. From then on, I collected pictures of beautiful baby boys and made a scrap book of them. I even bought a huge poster of a very beautiful baby and posted it on the wall of my bedroom.

My Own Baby Boy

One year later, I was twenty, and I gave birth to my firstborn. It was such a joy beyond compare when I first set eyes on him. It was like I fell in love for the first time. I just couldn't believe I had my own baby coming out from me. Then in my solitude I had resolved quietly, and with tears of joy in my eyes, that from this day onward my life would revolve around him. He was a bulky twleve-pound baby boy, so big for a Filipino infant at birth. He was also so fair skinned for a Filipino baby that people around would say that his father must have been a Caucasian. He was the most beautiful baby I had ever seen, and he was my son, my gift from God. He was more beautiful than those in the pictures I had collected. Such an awesome feeling beyond description.

The Reality of Parenting

But the awesome baby is another human being, and the responsibility of being a parent is not just to awe in wonder in every moment of the child's life. I realized in my youthful motherhood that to have a child is in fact the onset of a completely changed life. I took this realization seriously so I sat down one day and wrote everything that my new life should be with my child in my full charge. I listed scenarios of our life together in a moment-by-moment basis, including the life of my baby since birth up to the time that he would be the father of my grandchildren.

One Sunday when I was attending church, the preacher told of five brothers who all became pastors when they were adults. Their dad was a judge and was so disappointed because he should have wanted another judge or attorney from any of his sons. This message gave me an idea

The Only Rule Is LOVE

I love my baby every second, every minute, every hour, every day, every week, every month, every year, and for the rest of my life. The bottom line is I love him unconditionally and with the kind of love that only a mother's heart can do. The question then is, how do I love my child? Because I love my child, I formulated the following scenario:

1. I will finish my degree (I was out of school then) so that he will be proud of me when he grows up.

2. I will make him a millionaire son when he is in his twenties. But how could it be when I am not a millionaire myself? I knew then that I was just hitting the moon, but I did research works just for this obsession, the obsession of a young mother in love with her firstborn. I wanted the best for him, and if I could not help him in the outward deeds, at least I could do mental activities to make this dream for my son come true.

However a mother wants the best for her child, the child as an independent entity has a mind of his own that might be different from a mother's mind. The only rule that applies here is to love the child, that kind of love that respects the child's desire for himself. But I still had some methods that would not make him feel like he was being pushed to do what he did not want.

My Strategy as a Doting Mother

While life was busy with work, dreams, ambitions, plans, and every concern there was in life, my priority was still my son, and my daughter who followed three years later. Having two beautiful children made me more inspired in life. I finally finished my degree.

Things I did for their future success

1. Big posters on the wall that could mold their characters
2. Musical instruments
3. Scrapbooks and coloring books
4. Spending quality time as a family
5. Giving them assignments and rewards for achievement

Big posters on the wall.

My objective for the posters is to have a successful son and daughter in their adult life, so in my son's bedroom I had beautiful and colorful posters of a wealthy and famous personalities. Other posters were of money. I also created a collage that showed me as being wealthy with all the symbols of money and success. In the receiving room and all around the walls of my house were posters of guitars and musical instruments because I wanted my son to be a good guitar player just like my dad and brother.

<u>Musical instruments</u>. Music is the language of the soul and so aside from the posters of musical instruments, I bought guitars and electronic organs that I played myself. I also invited my brother to play the guitar and eventually encouraged my son to play it.

<u>Scrapbooks and coloring books</u>. I didn't really push them with colors and scrapbooks; I just bought a lot of them and did coloring myself. The objective was to model to them what I wanted them to be. I drew and colored and he just imitated me until he became a good painter. Most of my drawings were of nature, but the scrapbooks were money and material possessions.

<u>Spending quality time/giving rewards</u>. Spending quality time with kids differs in many ways. It can be educational, leisurely or playfully, exploring nature, excursions in the city or some establishments, and the church. These could be done spontaneously, better yet as a surprise or reward for good works in their parts.

Parenting is a lifetime job. Parents learn from their children and vice versa. There might be some conflicts along the way, but I believe in "problems resolve themselves," that is, if love rules in the mother-child relationship, and in all relationships.

I Am: "I Think Therefore I Am"

March 7, 2017

I AM SHARING HERE THE philosophy of existence...let those who have brains understand, those who have eyes see, and those who have ears hear...

"I Think Therefore I Am." I borrow this statement of Rene Decarte for the title of this hub. This hub is actually a poem I created springing out from the bottomless vacuum of human existence. The title of this poem is "I Know You."

I Know You

You authentically exist, I acknowledge you; in fact, you had been
    long in existence eons before I came out to this physical world;
The wind carried you swiftly with a lightning speed from nowhere
    through all the four dimensions of the universe and the four
    corners of this globe;
You were there very long before the Great Wall of China was
    conceptualized by those who came to and went off in the land
    of the living;
You watched the advent of civilization and how it flourished in the
    Nile as it advanced toward the so-called New Age of human
    existence;

You are lulled to sleep by the melody of angels singing their praises of love and beauty to the "Alpha and Omega," the Almighty no-beginning and no-ending HIM;

In the Land of Nowhere where the universe dances and sings with the myriads of bejeweled stars and the whole of the planetary family, you are there too, celebrating festively;

You swim and wade in the infinitely wide and deep blue oceans of the endless depths somewhere, yes somewhere;

The seven times heat of Nebuchadnezzar's oven is nothing compared to your billions and trillions and even measureless voltage;

You are Omniscience, everywhere and anywhere, every time and anytime, somewhere and someway, and anyhow and anyway;

You are clad with the infinitely colored brilliant beauty and the glaring gleam of once upon a time Lucifer's priceless gems;

Your Being You is beyond telling by any fallible human like me but I know you.

In all of your wanderings and adventures with the brightness and brilliance of everything sprouted and created and with the timelessness of your perfectly aesthetic existence, one day you came to a halt, an impossibly abrupt halt;

You were suddenly tasked for a mission to accomplish in order to prove the authentic relevance and purpose of your existence;

The Order came to you as a complex mixture of complete and lingering darkness, a thunderous and boisterous sound of the unknown and the nowhere, a lightning speed and glare from a throne beyond the blue;

You are trapped!

You stumbled to the abyss of no escape;

Escapade is only possible when the mission is accomplished with flying colors of honor and glory;

Or you can hate your situation enough to abort the mission of your own volition;

No rewards for such choice, only punishments; for forever you will be disdainfully ugly and be eternally exiled to the infamous cell of eternal imprisonment and damnation for the King of Tarsus, the once upon time Lucifer, whose choice was to reign on the throne of endless discomfort, to say the least;

Countless of the inhabitants there were like you and they made their choice to go against the Will, against the Order;

You are vacuumed in confusion; You want to scream but to whom? You want to move but how?

This is a totally different ground you are in; Your power is limited in this vacuum;

You needed to be connected to the Land of Nowhere where you have been;

You are trapped inside the Crown of Creation, Me!

A lot of those like me do not acknowledge the likes of you in them, and it bothers me a lot;

I want to reach out to them and tell them to take heed to the one who dwells in them;

How can I be understood?

But you must be persistent inside me;

Your scream within me is so loud, you won't let me sleep unless… unless, I recognize you and listen to you;

I listen to you and I have been listening since I acknowledged your authentic existence in me;

I know you because you are Me.

I Chose to Live; Not Just Exist

March 8, 2017

HARMONIOUS RELATIONSHIPS WITH OTHER HUMANS, even with animals, with money, and with any objects, is an integral part of truly living a fulfilling life rather than just existing and drifting in life without direction. To live is to be in an inspiring relationship with everything that you deem important in your life to live with.

Here's a poem dedicated to my husband. Dedicated to the love of my life.

I Chose You

I choose to live, not just exist;
To live is to move on, I move on;
To live is to grow and be fruitful, I grow and am fruitful;
To live is to be creative, I am creative;
To live is to be productive, I am productive;
To live is to prosper, I continuously prosper;
To live is to enjoy the fruit of your labor, I enjoy the fruit of my labors;
To live is to share the blessings, I share my blessings;

Life is abundance and happiness, I am abundance and happiness; Because I chose to live not just exist.

I choose to love you, not just to settle for anyone who is interested in me; To love you is to gladly share myself and my all to you, so I give myself and my all to you; To love you is to merge my soul, my heart, my mind, and my bodily pleasure with you; so I do just that; To love you is to completely accept you as you are unconditionally; so I do just that; To love is to forgive and to appreciate the goodness in you; so I do just that; To love you is what I live for; I choose to live; Therefore I chose you.

Depressed? Try This Antidote Imagery

March 9, 2017

Ideal Scene

I am just lying so relaxed on my sweet-smelling, soft, and silky bed. I am now slowly and unthinkingly sliding my palms on the silky bed cover while my mind wanders on those beautiful things I would like to posses if I have enough money. I have one hundred of them on my unwritten list of those wonderful things I would spend on, if my resources allow me. Suddenly, my cellphone rings; it is on top of the side table of my bed. Its ring abruptly brings me back to my present situation. I grab it and say, "Yes? Hello?" The voice in the other end asks me to confirm my identity, in which he mentions my name. All I say is, "Yes." Then his litany starts by saying, "You just have won $100M tax-free..." and continues with the details on why and how to get it. I have no idea how long such a phone call lasts, but when I hang up the phone I go back to my original situation calmly, lying on bed and continue imagining spending on all those things that I want to posses, do, and become. Now that I have all the money I could ever use for everything that my mind can afford to imagine, my imagination becomes intensified with the surety of the present reality. The imagination now becomes a necessity and comprehensive. I start writing down what to do in a very detailed manner and with feelings. What I see in this fantastic vision is that I get myself ready by using my most expensive bath soap and shampoo in my shower. Humming a tune as I shower and while my mind is seeing my hands touching and counting the bulk of dollar bills. Then I wear my favorite dress, the one that make me feel like a superstar and very attractive, fix my hair, and relish the beauty and fashionable me in front of the mirror. I see the happy smile on my face as I try to remain calm. From the mirror I stand up and put on my favorite shoes and pick my favorite handbag. Then I start down the stairway as I call my driver to pick me up and wait on me for the whole day. The bank is my first destination. Here I spend two hours to get all the money matters set. My $100M is now in my personal account, and I can get the cash or check in any amount that I desire to spend in any given time. I am rich! A multimillionaire! I am lucky! I am a winner! I am blessed! And all these sorts of thoughts affirming my reality are now screaming loudly within me. On the outside, though, I am just all smiles and glow to express my happiness at the least. From the bank, my driver takes me to my favorite and expensive restaurant. In the restaurant I choose a strategically situated table in a conference or private room. Once there, I tell the waiter to bring me the specialty food for the day as an initial order. Then I start on my phone by calling the most important people on my horizon.

List of people to call: Greg, my husband; Rhena Jean, my daughter; Sunny, my son-in-law; Ma'am Veron, my best friend; Che-Che, my niece; Joy, the long-time nanny of my grandchildren; Reynan, my son; Mimie, my daughter-in-law; Popo (Rhenzl), my eldest granddaughter; Moj and Pokoy (Rhea Cezil and Rhon Caezar), my twins teen grandchildren.

There would be more later, but they live too far away for an instant dinner or lunch. To each of these people on the list I would say, "Whatever you do now, leave it. Come and join me in my celebration for winning

$100M. You will receive $10,000 gift once you are here to partake of the dinner with me in this celebration." My driver fetches them, and in less than one hour all of them are surrounding me. All of us are happy and far richer.

Aftermath and happy ever after I am now living a happy and fulfilling life. I had actually gifted my daughter with money more than enough for her to buy a house and lot and a car plus an investment for whatever business she would like to venture, likewise with my son. Whereas, aside from helping my friends, family, and distant relatives, I have the following list to spend on:

1. Spend the rest of my life with my husband, traveling the world, hotel hopping and cross-country hopping together

2. Buy ourselves a dream house in the Caribbean or anywhere in America where the weather and environment could help keep us healthy, youthful, and energetic all year round

3. Buy ourselves a dream car that fits our new lifestyle and personality

4. Create something that we both are interested in doing and be productive. The list could continue to the details of one hundred items.

The concept: A study conducted by Psychologist David Schultz with patients of depression at Yale and West Haven, Connecticut VA Hospital showed that depression could be reduced by visualizing cheerful scenes such as winning a lottery and other appealing ideal scenes for the person concerned.

William James said, "The greatest discovery of my generation is that human beings, by changing the inner attitudes of their minds, can change the outer aspects of their lives."

And Napoleon Hill also said this popular adage: "Whatever the mind of man can conceive, it can achieve."

Now go ahead, "if you can imagine it, then you can create it." as William Arthur Ward says. Create your own appealing imaginings in a cheerful spirit, if only to divert yourself from the harsh reality surrounding you. Be sure to get into that trance-like state of relaxation, for focus and who knows...for manifestation?

Dear God: A Supplication to the Universal Force

03/10/17

THERE ARE TIMES IN OUR lives that we find ourselves angry and feeling hatred toward some people and situations that have caused us harm, hence, draining our energies. Anger is a very powerful feeling that, if not controlled, will cause us so much trouble. When left unresolved it can accelerate to hatred, which can then lead to behaviors to avenge ourselves that could hurt others too, even the innocent ones. Even the Bible says, "Love your enemies...," a statement that is so hard to follow and which most people can only pretend. This kind of feeling happens when we feel we are being mistreated and being betrayed by the very people who are supposedly important to us. The negative feelings multiply and can eventually block the blessings that should have been intended for us, so life become a curse. Following is a prayer that can help us ease this feeling. This is also a prayer for protection so that nobody can hurt you and your feelings. Let God and the natural laws of the universe do what is good for you when you are pestered by this kind of destructive emotional state.

Dear God,

Heavenly Father, where are You? I feel so lost, but I remember Your promise to me being Your precious child in this universe that You created and love.

In my meditations, I clearly "hear" Your voice saying, "Ask of me and
I will give you whatever your heart desires."

In You, oh Lord, do I put my wholehearted trust;

Uphold me in Your Loving-Kindness;

Pamper me in Your Infallible Righteousness, and catapult me to a
safe ground.

Incline Your ears to my woes and let me experience Your Divine
Guidance.

You are my Strength, my Pillar, and my Stronghold;

My Rock, my Fortress, and my Refuge whose powerful words
command the whole Universe to protect me from harm.

Save me, oh God, from the claws of the wicked;

Snatch me from the hands of blood thirsty men whose days are spent
on self-destruction and causing misery to others in the process.

You are my All-knowing Almighty Father who upholds me even
when I was in my mother's womb;

You brought me out to this life to channel Your Divine Love to those
around me;

You are my Hope and Assurance in my youth;

You are always here within me and with me at every twist and turn
in my life's pathways;

I honor and glorify You in my mind, in my heart, in my soul, and in
my whole life through;

You are my Foundation; All praises to You, Heavenly Father, for as
long as I live.

I am my earthly father's delight and my mother's angel;

I am a wonder to many who know me personally;

All these are only true because You are my Father in Heaven who
empowers me;

Because You are a Living Fountain in my heart;

You actually live the life that I am living now;

My wisdom is Yours;

My words are Yours in my mouth;

My love for my loved ones and humanity as a whole is Your love for
them that You allow me to live upon;

In my whole life, all praises are for You, my Father in Heaven;

You stand by me and protect me when my faith in life and men fails me.

Where I am weak, You are my Strength.

My enemies may speak evil against me; they prowl and betray me;

They lie to me with their devilish schemes and they counsel among
themselves against me saying, "Her God has forsaken her; let's
pursue and shame her for there is none to save her."

But vengeance is Yours, my Father;

You know who they are and where You find them;

Let them be confounded and consumed;

Oh my God! Make haste to avenge me!

Let those who seek to hurt me, be filled with reproach and dishonor.

But for me, I will praise You and honor You more and more
continuously throughout my life;

My heart rejoices with the melody of Your angels voices that ring
deep in my soul;

My mouth shall only speak and tell of Your Great Faithfulness and
Your pure Righteousness all the days of my life;

I always live my life in the Strength and Power of my Almighty
Father;

The Strength and Righteousness of the Lord endures forever;

His Righteousness protects me against the evildoers.

Oh God! You had taught me Righteousness even in my youth;

To this day and to all the coming days that You had made for me, I
declare Your wondrous works in my life.

In my old days You fill me with your wisdom and power beyond fallible human understanding;

They can only surmise on Your Godhead and Righteousness, but are they there yet?

Their ignorance, disbelief, and dishonor to Your Power bring suffering as a consequence.

Your Righteousness, O God, is very high;

You perform miracles in my life;

Had shown me great wonders;

You lift me up to the highest pedestal in my life's station;

You bring me peace when I should have been in the den of the devil;

You snatched me out from the brink of death and hell;

You continuously and untiringly increase my greatness and comfort me in every twist and turn of my way;

With the music in my heart and with the melodious pulse beats of my blood, I praise Your Faithfulness to me, oh my Heavenly Father.

My God! You are my miracle.

The unfathomable Love of my life.

You lift me up above the ordinary;

My tongue speaks only Your Truth and Your Righteousness all the days of my life.

I praise You, oh God, for avenging me from the lying tongues and the evildoers;

They are now confounded and they cause themselves disgrace, dishonor;

Humiliation is their destiny.

Oh God! Who is like You in my life?

I Dream the Impossible

March 11, 2017

To LIVE IS TO DREAM, and to dream is to live. A person who stops dreaming has lost his direction in life. Dreams are inspirations for anyone to continue living despite life's hardships. Those who know me from my earlier days know that I am a dreamer. I remember the time when I was jobless and was just sulking inside my bedroom for a year after the death of my husband. My bedroom wall was all covered with posters that represented my dreams would all come true. Sunny, the husband of my daughter, was just dating my daughter at that time. He happened to enter my bedroom because my daughter told him to get something from my bedroom. When he was inside my bedroom he noticed all those posters on the wall. Later he commented to my daughter, "Your mom is a dreamer even at her age (I was fifty at that time; his parents were five years younger than me). I've never heard or noticed any such thing from my own parents. They feel like they are too old to dream..." Sunny's parents are now both deceased. When you stop dreaming you are just trying to convince your psyche that there is nothing in life anymore to look forward to, and so you drift and your body gets sick and tired of living. Life is a dream, and to live is to continue dreaming and pursuing such dreams. I am an avid believer of dreams come true.

Now that I am here in America, my close friends in the past would message me on Facebook that my dream of marrying an American and living here in the United States has finally come true for me. It's been my longtime dream, and I started dreaming this even when I was still married to my first and second husbands, and I had expressed my dreams to them. When you dream do not expect or do anything to make your dreams come true; just live your life on a moment-by-moment basis and accept yourself and the situation as is, but always be happy for the fact that you can still dream. One very important rule in creating a dream is to dream the impossible; dream those things that you think are impossible because you don't know how to make it happen given your situation. It's free to dream, so make it big. When you dream of money don't just dream of say $10,000 to pay your bills and rent or buy some particular thing. Dream of infinite amounts of money. Why not dream of something that you know how to make happen? If you know how to make it happen, then you are not dreaming; you can just do it, like maybe get a loan that in turn will give you more financial difficulties later. When you dream "small dreams" you won't be happy when that happens, but imagine that you dream the impossible and it happened. Wow! The excitement is beyond measure. Life and living would be a wonder, so even in your dream see yourself happy. And for sure, dreams do come true; just learn the methods of the effective way to dream. Following are examples of my impossible dream. I would not like to know how this is going to happen, but I know that I won't die yet before these dreams find their way to my life.

It's Free to Dream!

One day in 2003, six months after the demise of my husband, I was inside a Rav4 car driven by my driver in the middle of the metropolitan Manila. There were high-rise condominiums across the six-lane busy central highway to Mega SM Mall. Jojo, my student, and her sister were with me too; we were to go shopping for some decors for my new condo. The driver parked the car near a twenty-four-story empty condominium. I first noticed that the condominium was finished, but there were no occupants yet, so I said jokingly, "They don't like my condominium... nobody lives here." Jojo did not get my humor. She actually thought that I was co-owner of the new building, but the driver said, "It's free to dream."

I Believe in Dreams Come True

I am a dreamer. When I was a child and in my teens, I imagined those things that I desired to become, to do, and to have. My dreams were actually realistic. What made them seemingly impossible was because I didn't know how to make them happen and they seemed so impossible to come true given my actual situation at the moment. I never made any effort to make my dream come true because my mind just couldn't see the "how." I just dreamed and was happy "inside" my dream. It is amazing to note that most of those I dreamed came true. Everything just happened, even those things that were seemingly impossible. I believe in dreams.

The Impossible Dreams I Dream Now

I dream of becoming a millionaire. Who does not?

I imagine that money comes to me easily and effortlessly in an avalanche of abundance. Money loves me and it comes flying down to me out of nowhere. Money settles down at my feet and kneels down before me, begging me to pick it and accept it into my life in great abundance. I don't care how I will become a millionaire; it's the job of the universe to dance with the music of my soul. I am just happy that I am alive and I can live in another world, the world of my dreams. I just know that one of these days, money will knock on my door and be delivered to me in an infinite amount. I won't think of how I am going to become a millionaire because then it would be impossible. My limited knowledge and resources will reject the idea, but it's free to dream. That's all I know. If I dream of winning the lottery, I will be stuck in thinking of what numbers to bet. If I dream of getting paid in millions from a talent well-presented or a job well-done, then that is another impossible thing to happen because I will just be paid according to my limited capability. So I will just dream this is the only thing I know how to do and send my dream to the universe, the universe that keeps all the treasures in its bosom.

I dream of becoming a best-selling author.

I still have no idea what to write and how this is going to happen, but I know that I will become one, not because I am the best but because I dream of it. Again, I send my dream to the universe who knows what's best. I am just awaiting the idea and the inspiration. I believe that once an idea is born and I nurture it, the opportunity will present itself.

I dream of owning and living in a mansion like this.

I imagine myself living like a queen in the castle with my husband as my king. We have servants to do the chores and maintain beauty and cleanliness in our home. We are living in opulence. I see myself having a sophisticated studio for my art works, my writing, my library, my show or exhibit room for my works, and my study room. Everything in my surrounding is spacious and a state of the art. Again, I don't know how this is going to happen. What is important is that I have a mind that can dream. The universe will take care of the rest.

I dream of becoming a celebrity in my own right.

I have always been popular in my family, my relatives, my school, and wherever I went. I don't exactly know why it was so; this is perhaps the reason why I have this dream of becoming a celebrity. I imagine myself being interviewed on a TV show, if it is only just for once. And again, I have no idea how and for what reason I will become one. I just dream and "submit" my dream to the universe and it's up to "it" as to how it is going to happen. My only role is to dream because I got the mind that knows what and how to dream.

My romantic heart finds the love of my life. One of those impossible dreams that came true to me.

I dreamed of finding my soul mate. I have been married twice, plus one live-in fiance, but my heart was still longing for my perfect match even while I was still married to my ex, and my late husband, God forgive me. I knew that they were not the ones I desired, so I drew my heart's choice, dreamed of him, and described his personal qualities and qualifications, and then sent my dream to the universe. Who would think that this dream came true? I dream the impossible...do you?

Just keep on dreaming. God knows which of your dreams will come true, and you will congratulate yourself for a job well done for every impossible dream that has come true.

Two Inner Reflections:
My Thoughts and My Prayer

March 12, 2017

Only Good Thoughts Dwell in My Mind

I wrote two powerful reflections on January 16, 2001. I say powerful because they really worked for me. It was a time in my life when my husband was bedridden and on oxygen. I knew it wouldn't be long before he went back to the Creator, but I needed strength to sustain me as I took care of him. He died two years later. If I reflect now how I did it, I can see the enormous strength I had to take care of him full time, leaving my job and care-giving from the smallest details till the end, for three years.

My Thoughts

Moment by moment, second by second;
Minute by minute, hour by hour;
Day by day, night by night;
Week by week, month by month; in every tic-tock of the clock is a
    moment of thoughts.
Now, this moment, is my only and perfect time for thinking of
    everything that is fine;

I think good and of good things only;

I think of good feelings;

I think of love and compassion;

I think of joy, delight, and pleasure;

I think of all natural beauties;

I think of God, the Source of "all things bright and beautiful"

I think of abundance and riches in this wonderful Universe;

I think of forgiveness and peace;

I think of the goodness in humans;

I think of all the pleasant and comforting words, live them, and speak them;

I think of good deeds for myself and for others;

I think of my service for my Lord and for all His creatures who need me;

I think of myself as God's channel of love and infinite creative energy and wisdom;

I think of all the wonderful things in this Universe and of riches untold;

I think of all the mysteries in the secret chambers of man's existence that are yet to unfold;

I think of all that man can think and create;

I think of all the wonders of man as God's "crown of creation" and masterpiece;

I think of God's unconditional love to all mankind;

I think of everything good that is manifesting to me this very moment;

I think and I think, and no matter how I think, I know that my mind never stops thinking, so I choose what I must think;

And these are only good thoughts for the good of all concerned.

These are my thoughts, this very moment.

My Prayer

Give me a heart that knows no ill;

Give me a clean and pure heart, oh Lord;

Impute in me the mind that thinks only good for everyone and for myself;

Grant me understanding, discernment, and wisdom;

Endow me with a healthy and strong body that reflects Your own and that can be of service for the weak and the weary.

Reflect in me Your love, kindness, and compassion for my children, my loved ones, and for those who are bereft of the essence of life's joy;

Inculcate in me peace, meekness, mercy, and grace to model your Greatness in my everyday life;

Let me fathom life's reality;

Allow me to envision creativity and presence of mind to model a fulfilling life;

Unfold me to the peak of my God-given energy and enthusiasm in order to accomplish and achieve my life's goals and purpose;

Empower me with a systematic and logical approach to life's challenges that I may meet along life's journey.

I praise You, oh Lord, for all the good things that You let me partake;

I count all my blessings, piece by piece, with such rejoicing in my heart;

I acknowledge You as the only Source of everything that I enjoy in life;

You granted me all the desires of my heart and You continue to fulfill Your promise of meeting all my needs in perfect timing at all times;

Whatever I asked in Your name is done unto me;

How Great You are in my life, oh Lord;

I desire to proclaim You and Your Goodness to those who are yet in the dark;

You are the Light when my path is cloudy;

You carry me with Your powerful arms when I am unable to move on my own;

My faith in You gets stronger as You continue to show me the wonders of living;

You reveal to me what is hidden beneath the seeming catastrophe of life;

Great is Your Faithfulness Oh Lord!

What You have done for me in the past is the same today and through eternity;

You have given me everything to live a fulfilling life in all areas;

Whatever I ask and pray for is already granted me, and even those I have not thought of asking due to my limited vision, You have already given me.

How Great You are, oh my Lord!

I humbly offer myself and my life to You, my Lord, just as I am;

I give You my mind, my heart, my body, and and all that I am;

I give You my love, my faith, my trust, my loyalty;

There is nobody else in this vast universe who is worthy of my praises and thanksgiving;

For I know that You have given Yourself to me even before I was conceived in my mother's womb;

And You are the Source of my life, which I gladly offer to You in return;

Make me Your trustworthy steward to perform the task You assigned me in this life;

Let me execute my talent in full capacity;

Mold me into a channel of Your Divine Love and Power;

Let me be the inspiration for others to live their lives according to
their individual Divine purpose;

I do everything for Your glory and honor, oh Lord.

I now claim the blessings that You intend for me today.

Thank you, Father.

These do I pray. Amen! And Amen!

"There Are No Tyrants if There Are No Slaves"; There Are No Bullies if There Are No Gullible

March 13, 2017

HUMAN BEINGS ARE GULLIBLE IN certain and varied degrees; otherwise, one is not human at all or he will be ineducable, worse than being gullible, isn't it?

Also in life and at every stage of development and socialization process, we sometimes stumble into a group for any reason. Then we meet people who impact our self-esteem and values formation. Unless you know the principles behind these relationships, you will feel like you are an outcast if you allow yourself to be the victim of circumstances. Life would then be greatly affected to the point that some would commit suicide or would avenge themselves that they become criminals in the extreme situation.

One significant reason for being gullible is the fact expressed in the statement: "No man is an island." People learn from other people in the process of socialization, beginning from the smallest unit in society, which is the family, peer groups, and so on, as he continues life's journey. What one becomes is the totality of his socialization processes and his inherent personal qualities. How one perceives and reacts to certain people and relationships, incidents and situations, location and territory, weather or environment, and so forth, comprise the accumulated type of personality one has become.

Reactions to all these life experiences also depend on the inherent mental attitudes and intellectual capacity of an individual. The degree and quality of interactions with all of these life situations also affect the growth and development of a person in every stage. These are just some of the many complexities a human experiences and what he becomes, a bully or a gullible?

The treatment one receives and perceives in the family setting at an early stage of development depends a lot on the personality composition of an individual. For example, being the first baby, son or daughter, with normally loving parents is favorable to the social standing of such a child. Of course this position has to come with the personal inherent qualities, such as beauty, health, intellectual capacity, talents, perceptions, speaking skills, etc.

All these personality components determine the quality of socialization an individual experiences in all his developmental stages in life and determines his position in society.

How One Becomes a Bully or a Gullible Victim

There are many and varied determinants, like what I had stated above, for one to become a bully. Given all those favorable and unfavorable social interactions from the smallest unit of society and, as he lives onward in the developmental processes, in addition to the inherent gene or nature of the person, a bully must have had unfavorable, even inhuman, treatment in his foundation years, or perhaps he is just a naturally rotten piece of a gene or both.

What Is Common to Both?

Similarly, such conditions apply to a gullible, or the victim of a bully, with the apparent reasons that one is a victim and the other the oppressor. Common to both is the unfavorable treatment or a perceived unfavorable as being inculcated to them from the family. Unfavorable treatment is broad, which includes violence to the extreme and overprotected on the other end, plus the inherent mental attitudes, tendencies, perceptions, and other mental capacities on the individual level.

Like Attracts Like

Not everybody is a bully or a victim of bullies. Given this premise, why would anyone become a victim, to the point of being killed by bullies? The answer would most probably be "like attracts like" and/or they reciprocate and need one another in order to survive in a world that these two types of personalities perceive as a tough life. This is something to ponder both for bullies and victims of bullies.

Purging and Clearing Techniques

March 14, 2017

Do you wonder why no matter how you follow the techniques I have presented, nothing still happens and there are no changes in your situation? The techniques of affirmation, collage, and drawings are very effective to manifest your desires only, and only if you are clear from anything that blocks your energy to reach your subconscious mind or that psyche that makes things possible for you.

Purging and Clearing Technique

These two words may sound strange for some readers, but in this article I am modeling a type or technique of clearing your hearts, minds, and souls from the spiritual, emotional, and psychological rubbish that you may have accumulated and stocked over the years in your "mental cabinet," thus blocking your energy from manifesting what you really desire and deserve to happen in your life.

Do you often wonder why no matter how you try or do your best you just fail to get what you really want or to actualize your dreams or to achieve your goals? Situations in your life such as financial difficulty, entangled relationships, nonchallenging job, and even some perennial feelings of emptiness continue to repeat in a spiral manner in every turn of your life. These repeated and continuous nuances should be cleared out and completely eradicated from your life in order for you to develop toward the completion of your being here in this life. Life should be lived and be alive rather than just going along struggling and coping with whatever comes your way till the end.

Living your life is a process and a series of choices from the smallest daily decisions, such as whether to say yes or no and what dress to wear when a friend suddenly invites you to an unannounced casual dinner or a major decision such as whether to abort an unwanted pregnancy or to keep the pregnancy going for nine months. These major decisions can change your life completely, because such a decision could lead to another major decision affecting your job, income, relationships, etc. Life should not be a continuum of a "problem-solving" nature; rather, it should be a continuous series of "creative" nature where every moment is a moment of creativity and a wholesome exploration and adventure in all areas.

No matter how seemingly brilliant and successful a person is in all his endeavors, if this rubbish is vacuumed in his core, then the time will come that it will just be one more "miss-take" for him and everything he has worked hard for will blow up and tumble down before his eyes.

Given the preceding argument is valid, the following are two of some actual effective techniques I used in the spirit of fun; I am still using these when necessary:

1. Clearing through forgiving technique
2. Purging via inner exploratory conversation.

Forgiving Technique: Writing a Letter

In this technique, I write down the name of the person who hurt me today or yesterday or in the nearest past, one person at a time. Then I write him a letter. The following is a simple example:

George, (husband)

You hurt me deeply. You yelled at me and called me an idiot, an ignorant, and worse you lie to me and betray my trust in you. You cheat on me by having an affair with another woman, yet you continue to lie and deny your wrong doings. Your betrayal to our marriage vows hurt me to the core and is draining my energy, having lost my enthusiasm to function normally.

But now I have made the decision. I am dissolving all these restricting energies that block me from my personal progress. I have to forgive you. I am forgiving you now. I forgive you and I let go of all the blocks between us. I forgive you now; go your way as I go mine. I now bless you.

Then I read the letter as I ponder on its truthfulness, feel the hurt in the area where the hurting point is mentioned, and allow myself to cry if I feel like crying. Then I feel the relief where the letting go is mentioned. Finally, I tear the letter and burn it or throw it to the rubbish as a gesture of completion, then forget about it. Having accomplished something brings a feeling of relief.

Purging: Inner Exploration

In this technique, I am writing down an inner conversation with myself concerning matters that are bothering me in the present. I have named my inner self Senotiza. The following is an example of our conversation:

"Me (Jenny): Senotiza, what's bothering me?

S (Senotiza): Hmmm, no formal address to me? Can't you be a bit polite?

Me: I don't even want to live anymore (expletives if you wish), what can being polite do with my disgusting life now?

S: At least be civil.

Me: Sh...(expletive) answer my question.

S: And if I won't?

Me: And why won't you? What's the use of your existence in me?

S: Hey, Jenny, what's boiling you now?

Me: I am so mad because I bought some lottery tickets today and I never won anything.

S: Wowooo! Lottery tickets huh!

Me: Yes, because I want to be a multimillionaire.

S: Hehehe...hahhaahahahah...aren't you being funny?

Me: Sh...don't laugh at me, I am serious!

S: Serious in winning the major lottery jackpot or serious in becoming a multimillionaire? C'mon stop kidding me.

Me: Both, I want to become a millionaire by winning the lottery.

S: In that case, you are limiting your chances to become a millionaire, whereas if it's the becoming a millionaire you focus on, you will have less frustrations.

Me: But I cannot think of any way to become an instant millionaire.

S: Just because you cannot think doesn't mean that there is no other way. What about just pretending that you are already a millionaire? By the way, why would you want to be a millionaire? What are you going to do with such huge amount of money?

Me: Hmmm...I just want to experience having plenty of money, something like no matter how I spend, and my money is still intact.

S: Could be but what if you got your wish granted? Do you have anything specific in your mind to spend on?

Me: Yes, first I will share my blessings with my daughter; she is now building a house so I'd love to contribute in the amount of P2M, then I also give her another P1M to buy her car and whatever she wants. I love my daughter and I want her to enjoy some goodness in life. Then my husband and I will travel within a year around the globe, hopping from one country to another, living in luxury hotels and resorts and meeting all my friends around the globe. I will introduce my husband to them. My husband has been working all his life and he is very generous to me; he deserves the goodness in life. I want him to spend the rest of his life with me full of joy and a fulfillment.

S: Hmmm…noble objective…go on, just continue imagining what you do with your money. I will be right back with some surprises for you.

There would be a lot of topics, more serious ones if you wish in this type of inner conversation. The idea is that you will discover what you really want and you will know from within you those things that are holding you back. It is okay to explore impossible areas. An idea or answer will just come out and you will be surprised when you will be open to many possibilities.

Just do this exercise in the spirit of fun. Life will never be boring once you have learned to adapt this technique in your daily life. The only rule here is just do it; don't ask questions.

Smile, Laugh, and Be Lucky

March 15, 2017

Do you laugh a lot? Why and what makes you laugh? Your own thoughts momentarily? Your feelings in that particular time? Or, is it anything you hear, see, touch, read, smell, or say that makes you smile at this certain moment? People are a bundle of varied and diversified emotions. These emotions may come in a surge or as a reaction to any given environmental stimulus in a particular time and situation or occasion.

All of us have experienced all these emotions at some point. Emotions are intangible but demonstrable through our behavior or action in a given moment. Some observable show of emotions may be smiling, laughing, crying, lashing, screaming, yelling, kissing, hugging, and the list can go on and on. Is it the company of someone you fully trust, love, care for, and with whom you have been familiar with for a long time that you just blurt into laughter spontaneously with just a slight provocation?

But the question is, of all the emotions you have experienced, which ones make you feel good about yourself, your relationships, and life as a whole? Or do you think that emotions have definite bearings on how your life is going in all areas?

How does a habitual spontaneous smiling and laughing attitude attract good luck?

1. Lady Luck cannot resist a merry heart. It's been said that: "Fortune is a lazy goddess; she will never come to you." But Lady Luck cannot resist a merry heart, and this merry heart must be loud enough for Lady Luck to hear, must be bright and glaring enough for Lady Luck to get curious about and be drawn to you, and must be a full-packed action of wholesome and habitual behavior for Lady Luck to stick with you.

2. Habitual and spontaneous laughter in intimate relationships magnetizes Lady Luck. Studies have shown that couples and family members who laugh a lot together for any reason, or even for seemingly no reason at all, are the ones who stick together and are inseparable. It's the laughter they share together in a habitual and spontaneous manner that draws them together even in the midst of difficulty, grief, and problematic situations. So you get "Lucky" in your relationships.

3. Lady Luck bows down to a persistently bright and shining smile and to a thunderous and spontaneous laughter. A person who notices any humor in little things in life can easily smile and laugh, hence, develop wholesome and bright dispositions even in a most difficult situation. So he gets "Lucky" eventually.

A Scenario

I am going to share some experiences here to prove my point, to show how my smile and laughter invited Lady Luck to my horizon. I was younger but already married with two children. My eldest, a son, was age seven and my daughter, the youngest, was age four. It was my first year of teaching in a public high school wherein new teachers received a monthly pay of P1,337. At that same time, I was also studying at MSU-IIT (Mindanao State University—Iligan Institute of Technology) taking up my MBA as a scholar. I used to drop by in my best friend's eatery before proceeding to my six-to-nine MBA p.m. MBA schedule. I had to have a quick snack; I was famished from my seven-to-five, eight-hour daytime teaching job. My best friend at that time was Becky; she owned and ran the Hamburger House. This was the place I frequented every day from 5–5:30 p.m. during the workdays and before proceeding to my MBA classes at MSU-IIT. Becky and I used to laugh a lot together, oblivious of whether people noticed our behavior. In one of my appearances there after school, Becky told me that two guys sitting at one of the tables wanted to be introduced to me. Naturally I declined; I was not good with strangers and I easily lashed out at people when a hint of disrespect dropped in my ears. But Becky, being my trusted long-time friend, assured me that these guys were decent and they just had to ask me some important questions. We had ten minutes of good introductions before I left for school. Before leaving, Engineer Recto, one of the two guys and who happened to be the superintendent in one of the departments in National Steel Corporation, told me, "Jenny, you got that winning smile and that sharp brain. Can we talk some time about a job offer in National Steel Corporation?" To this I answered, "Try me."

The job offer was a three-hour motivation lecture every Sunday. I was paid P1,500 per hour, which means I was receiving P4,500 every Saturday or P18,000 a month. Compared to my P1,337 per month salary teaching in public school, P18,000 was a fortune. And to top it off, I didn't have to leave my main job of teaching in a public school because I was only giving lectures for three hours on the weekend, a Sunday. It all just started with a smile and the habitual attitude of smiling, even with a slight provocation.

A smile conveys a positive vibes to the observers. The National Steel Corporation was the biggest steel corporation in Asia at that time, and I was employed as a motivational lecturer. This was just one of the many experiences of good luck in my life that started with just a smile.

So smile, laugh, and good luck.

A Letter to "Senotiza"

03/16/17

WRITING TO YOUR HIGHER SELF is one very effective technique to remind you of your self-value and to count the blessings and wonders that have happened in your life. Very often, people forget the blessings they have experienced and instead dwell on the painful experiences, thus making them perennial residents in their souls. This causes their lives so much misery. What I am discussing here is an example of how and what to write to yourself, the inner you who knows what you have been through, where you are now, and where your life's path is leading you. Senotiza is the name I designate to my higher self. Writing to one's higher self is one technique to assert self-value. Here's the letter I wrote to her:

Dear Senotiza,

Greetings to the most highly respected and honored essence of my total existence. It has been so long (and long is since I became aware of my being in this dimension called life) that I so desired to write to you.

There was a whole year in the past when I consistently wrote a letter per day to "God." I had collected a volume of notebooks reflecting every detail of my life during that period. In my letters to Him were everything that transpired in my life on a daily, hourly, and minutely basis.

The most significant results in that consistent writing activity to God for a year was the realization that all my requests and complaints in the deepest sense (deepest sense means that I was crying when I wrote them) were all answered. I noticed that all my worries and concerns were resolved in due time during the interim.

Such writing activity actually strengthened my faith to the Most Powerful Intelligence and Existence of Someone or Something beyond the scope of human discernment. Now, My Most Respected Senotiza, I am resolved to writing to you on a daily basis for a year. I hope you don't mind.

The decision to write to you after decades of not doing it, despite my intention, comes up because of two reasons, namely:

1. I now have the clarity of intention to pursue the dream that I have been hatching for a long time.
2. I have completely developed connectivity with you, and I have learned to acknowledge your presence in my life and to listen and accept your role as being one with me to live the life that is uniquely and perfectly just for me.

In this letter I have three basic points to discuss with you:

1. To establish and harness harmonious a relationship with you and to consult your wisdom about my present situation and onward

2. To invoke clearing, purging, and dissolution of cemented energy in my system that may have blocked me from a swift transformation to the life that I deserve
3. To appeal to your Pure Energy to enact and hasten the manifestations of my life's ideal scenes

Senotiza, you have been hinting to me of your presence, especially during the low times of my life. I have always been amazed at how problems resolved themselves at a time when I had given up all my best efforts. People around me with shallow understanding of the universal laws that govern this universe and its billions of replica including me, may despise and scorn me out of ignorance, but I know you are with me and have been with me all the way.

You never fail me. I may oftentimes forget or ignore you because of some pressing situations, but you always hint at me that you can do better if I listen to you and just follow your guidance. You never fail me and I am assured of this, but I am also aware that you require my patience and perseverance in major areas of my life while you are working at it. My only regret is sometimes you impose hibernation in my material calendar so that I sometimes blow up when I feel that the hibernation period has been prolonged beyond my line of patience. But I have learned to trust in you. This trust in you is demonstrated at the time when I face life bravely despite its mundane pressures. Pressures in my life in terms of relationships, job, money, health, dreams, goals, plans, and the fallible untrustworthy people who surround me, yet I can see that these are just incidentals in the process of developing and strengthening my trust in you.

How can I forget this one incident of my life where you took charge of the situation? I was bedridden for a week, literally with paralyzed arms and legs. I could not raise an arm to hold a coffee mug. I was shocked in disbelief. I knew it was the consuming grief of losing Colin that killed my desire to live. Nobody and nothing around me, including my children, could console me. There was just nothing left in life for me. I was homeless, jobless, penniless, had feelings of being abandoned and left out by my own children, and felt sick at heart and body; death was the only way out, out from this completely miserable state.

But out of the blue, the news of Escobar being in Angeles City set me on my feet. I instantly stood up as if nothing happened. Escobar, the Chilean Missionary who ordained my dad a long time ago, when I was barely ten years old. My dad sent me to the missionary field when I was fifteen under the guardianship of Escobar. Escobar had not visited the Philippines since he left in 1974. I last saw him when I was sixteen, at that lowest time of my life. He was looking for me, and then I followed the call for me to go back to teaching in SPCC with my best friend Ma'am Veron.

I started living again since then, alone but back to myself, Professor Senotiza. These are just among the many "miracles" or incidents that happened in my life during my lowest times; they are beyond explanation. You hint in me the assurance that "if nothing else works then, if necessary, the universe will summon literal angels to my rescue."

Senotiza, this letter is already very long, and I have tackled only the first area of the subject that I want to discuss with you. My next letter will be about the invocation for purging and clearing.

I acknowledge and appreciate so much your guidance and wisdom that continuously works in my life.

Respectfully,
Jenny

Labyrinth of Life:
A Moment-by-Moment Series of Choices

March 17, 2017

I AM NOW SIXTY-TWO YEARS old, a happy and proud grandma of seven awesome grandchildren. The lovable and cute eldest grandchild (a girl) is now an architecture graduate and is working as such in Manila. I am a mother of a young successful IT businessman who is the father of my five awesome teenage twins. I have a professional daughter who runs her own business and is a mother of two wonderfully beautiful kids ages seven and five.

That is the initial and general evaluation of my life; when I look back to review what I have been doing over the years and to reevaluate my decisions and choices at every turn, I am inclined to ask myself, Is everything that has happened my own choice? Is my situation now a dream come true and the destination that I had foreseen and worked on over the years toward its fulfillment? Do I like my life now? Could I have made it better than what I have now? What have I been doing in all the areas of my existence? Was I aware that I made the choices or decisions or did I just go with the flow on the river of life and cross my fingers to wherever my existence would land? Did I create the twists and turns of my life or did I exist in a dream-state of mind so that I found myself one day to be in the midst of a labyrinth? Or was I even aware that I was trapped in a certain labyrinth? If so, how did I manage to find my way out if I did, or am I still labyrinth hopping, thus just existing rather than living as a co-creator of a meaningful life that is meant just for me? Lots of questions! One question leads to more and more complicated ones. This is perhaps the reason why most of mankind just exists, not caring whether they just exist in a labyrinth or not, because life is so complicated to ponder on.

People just play the game of life, win or loss; it doesn't really matter. The winners spit on losers and the losers hate the winners, but "life" goes on and on and on. No need to think because thinking is tedious, while it is much easier to just follow the game of the day. The issue is to play the game inside the labyrinth, the hide-and-seek game of existence.

Lots of people ask: What is the purpose of life? Do you believe in the purpose of life? How will we understand life? Are there steps to follow in order to be happy in life? What is happiness? and so on.

Just like the fish inside a fisherman's net at sea, they continue swimming and enjoy their company while having no idea that they are already entrapped in a net and that in just a few seconds or minutes they will be a delicious menu on a plate to feed hundreds or thousands of ever-hungry humans.

Awareness and Assertiveness Are the Keys

Are you serious about your life: relationships, job, money, material possessions, or anything you value, to infinity? Of course, many talk about success in relationships, career success, financial success, health success, spiritual success, and so forth. It is easy to talk about all these. Head knowledge and statistics are easily accessible, but the question remains, how do you live your life now? Are there areas in your existence that need improvement and do you have any innovative ideas?

We are talking life here, and life is all we got. Without it that's the end of the story. Be aware and pay attention to what your self is telling you. Listen to that "still small voice" within you and listen well; it has messages on a moment-by moment-basis to guide you. Can you hear it? It holds the keys to your freedom from this labyrinth of existence.

Basic Things to Ponder and that Really Matter in Living One's Life

March 18, 2017

LET ME ASK A FEW questions that could possibly trigger our mental processes:

1. Have you ever wondered why you would want to continue living?

2. Is it something like you live because you have no choice… you were born so you have to continue living or existing till you die…or because you cannot just stop breathing or you just cannot kill yourself so you have no choice but to continue existing?

3. Next question is, do you really live or do you merely exist? What is the difference between mere existing and really living?

4. If you really live, then what is the meaning of life for you or what makes your life meaningful?

5. What are the things (whether you possess it already or that you are still pursuing) that you really value in your life?

Let me discuss each question. The answers here are my personal answers, and I am speaking for myself. Individual differences would cause millions of varied answers to the same questions, and everybody is entitled to live the life that one chooses.

Why Live?

Question number one reminds me of an incident with my dad some decades back when I was just entering puberty. My dad spanked me because he said I was stubborn. I cannot really recall in details why I made him so angry, but I remember my statement to him: "You should not have sired me; I wish I was not born."

I was sobbing as I said it, not only because of the physical hurt of the belt that he beat me on but worse was the agonizing feelings of inadequacy that made me feel like I didn't deserve to live because I was not good enough. I felt that I was a mistake, that I was born a mistake or that it was a big joke or mistake to be here in this life.

Question number two; I actually attempted to commit suicide many a times, but I found out that even in killing myself I was not good enough because no matter what I tried to do to kill myself I couldn't succeed.

For question number 3: We did not choose to be born, neither did our parents chose what kind of personality their children would be once they were born or what kind of life they would live (if they did live life.) In this statement, it is very tempting to discuss whether there was anybody who made the choice as far as our personalities and kind of life we would be living. The preceding argument would be deeper and broader topics to discuss so that I will just have to limit this discussion to the "now" that we are already in this dimension of the supposedly living state.

Assuming that we have to continue existing because "that's the way it is" and we are too coward (or brave enough?) to kill ourselves, then we have to let our ability to choose the kind of life to live for ourselves in order to really live that life in accordance to the intention of the Giver or Creator of all lives and things in nature.

To personally choose the direction of your life is life itself. This is the only way to live life, as opposed to just existing and being blown where the wind goes.

To Live and to Merely Exist

Basically we all exist whether we like it or not, regardless of what kind of existence each of us is going through. The majority of the people exist and can easily ride on the bandwagon of what everybody is doing or needs to do in a given time, place, society, or culture. If one would be good enough to belong and be like everybody else, then that would be enough for them and there would be fewer tensions to tackle.

The common pattern of life in a given society would be first, being born, then belong to the family, then belong to the peer group or age level socialization processes—church (if any), school, job, and so on. Some people do it well enough to be in that social pattern, but for various reasons a lot more cannot cope and adjust to this social pattern due to many individual differences (or social defects?). For instance, the IQ cannot cope with lessons in school, being bullied, financial difficulties, and many individual preferences and personal conflicts that cannot adhere to the requirements inherent in the pattern that a given society has sanctioned in its evolving nature.

Whether one can belong well to the societal sanctions or sidetrack from it, one basic human endeavor is to be happy in the kind of life he had chosen. If one has to be on the "bandwagon," then that must be his or her personal choice; likewise, if one is on the "sidetrack," then that must be his or her personal choice as well.

For question number four:Is happiness the meaning of life to you? Then pursue happiness whatever that means to you personally. Happiness then is living the life you have chosen and created for yourself and can be defined as the freedom to choose. Not only has that one known of this freedom but also to have one's freedom to choose work accordingly.

Simply put, freedom to choose the kind of life you desire for yourself and to achieve it within your capacity makes your life meaningful and worth-living.

Meaning of Life for You

Life can only be meaningful if you have defined it for yourself and acquired or achieved those things that you deem most important for you. This is so that you protect those things from any outward attacks that may damage the values you put into it. There are countless areas in life that one may value. The values put into these basic things may vary with individual preferences. Individual preferences are influenced by cultural, psychological, spiritual, physical, genetic, material, and other things in your background.

Among the many areas in life that an individual can value and which one is convinced that he cannot live without are:

1. Family
2. Relationships and the Socialization Processes
3. Education
4. Self-Expression
5. Socioeconomic Status or Status Quo
6. Travel and Leisure
7. Hobbies
8. Personality
9. Self-Value, Dignity
10. Spirituality

The preceding are just a few of the possible choices, out of millions, that an individual could be interested in and which one may value throughout his life.

What Is Your Trigger?

03/19/17

I MAY BE DEFINING THE word "trigger" here in a different light. I limited my definition to this word as a motivational technique I created for myself in order to enjoy at the same time that I pursued to materialize my dream or to achieve the goals that I created for myself. I believe in this statement: "The dreams of dreamers can lead to great achievements." Everybody is capable of dreaming for a better life or for anything that one desires for his or her life, but only a few have the ability to pursue and achieve their goals. Pure logical reasoning very often wears us down with obvious reasons why it is impossible to pursue such a dream, and so these dreams of such dreamers lie as a stillborn, never seeing the light of day. Trigger techniques make almost everything workable, therefore, possible. A trigger is a combination of physical action that the mind is aware of and agrees to follow as soon as the body does the agreed action; hence, it is physical or mental imagining or visualizing, as well as emotional, which must be done to achieve the desired result. I share the following techniques as examples; anyone can create his own specific techniques. I made the "action words" bold to give my readers the idea about what is to be done.

Techniques I use to trigger myself to eagerly do what I want:

1. Given my **love for writing**, I decide what outcome I want. This means that I love writing, but I can only write if in a given

moment I have nothing else to do and so every time that I have nothing else to do, I press my thumb which means I have to start writing. Hence when I realize I am not doing anything in a given moment **I press my thumb to remind me that I am ready to write. Then I start writing.**

2. I think of familiar things that I already enjoy doing or that which is of utmost importance for me, and this is what I write about; for example, **public speaking.** Having decided the desired outcome and having chosen the subject I am already motivated to write about, I imagine myself as follows: a.) writing or typing on my laptop; b.) looking at the typewritten words on the word-pad page as I am typing on it; c.) seeing my fingers move on the keyboards as I touch the letters to form the perfect words that I desire to convey; d.) hearing the clicking of the keyboards as I continue to type; e.) feeling the sensations inside me; f.) observing the clarity of my thoughts that flow in my creative mind; g.) while I am visualizing all these activities; h.) **I press down on my left knee;** this action creates a trigger, which is a one trial conditioned reflex that would call forth the sensations whenever I press my knee in the same way again.

3. Then I imagine myself speaking before an appreciative big audience. When I need to "feel again" the joy when I was speaking in front of an audience in the past, **I press my right knee. Now that makes two triggers.**

4. Then I apply the double-triggering technique to produce both sensations simultaneously. Double trigger means left and right knee pressing. In this case there has to be a preceding mental and action agreement to mean one thing.

5. Lastly, I mentally rehearse writing **Pressing my thumb.** I imagine myself writing in various places with this new eagerness I just created for myself. I also imagine myself as a successful author reaping the satisfactions and rewards of this achievement.

Now, what is your trigger? Try creating your own; it's fun and it works...trust me.

Episodes of Darkness

March 20, 2017

LIVING IS EMBRACING ALL OF life, the joys, the sadness, the pleasures, and the pains. Let's face it; life is not always bright and gay. In fact, it is full of confusion and gloom. Lots of those we dread are the ones that are in our immediate situation. We try to cope and shine to fade the shadows away. No effort is needed to be in the dark; you're just there. But to shine and to be in the Light requires constant and consistent alertness and assertiveness. The following is an expression of my feelings during a dark moment for some reason. Acknowledging your emotions, even the negative ones, will remind you that you are living your every moment and that you are capable of loving and accepting yourself no matter what. Following is an expression of my darkest moments. I entitle this "Leave Me Alone!"

> Leave me alone!
> Don't tell me you care for me
> All of you! Don't ask me where I have been and what I have been doing;
> Why do I have to explain defensively? You don't believe me anyway!
> You cannot and won't do what I want, why should I?
> I cannot tell you that I had gone to meet the Devil in Hades;

It's not fun to be with him, but his proximity is everywhere;

You can access him any moment any place. Just one misstep, one mistake, and he's there to meet you.

I should have desired to be in the glorious throne of the Heavenly King;

I should have loved to hear the voices of angels singing their hallelujahs to the Universal Power and the Almighty!

But it's too far away; I even have no idea where it is and can it be real?

Ha-ha, foolish people, foolish me! I don't care anymore;

I don't care about anything;

Leave me alone in my miseries;

Stop adding insults to my injuries.

Forget me if you will;

Remind yourself that I don't exist and never have been in your life.

Let me be a wanderer in the limbo of this so-called life of the living dead!

What Makes Everything Possible

March 21, 2017

ONE NIGHT WHEN MY GRANDSON was a fourteen years old, a grade IX student at the prestigious and expensive Ateneo de Cebu High School, he chatted with me on Facebook. His intro was "Hi, Lola (grandma), can I ask you a question?" To which I replied, "Yes, say it, Pokoy (that's my endearment for him, which means "my own beloved grandson"). His name is actually Rhon Caezar. He then proceeded to ask, "Do you believe that everything is possible?" I answered without hesitation, "100 percent yes." Then he said, "So you also believe that it is possible that some things are impossible."

Going back to the subject matter of this discussion: what makes everything possible? Everything is possible ONLY to those who are able and capable of making them possible. Hence, nothing is possible to anyone who cannot see even in their own minds the possibility of making a certain thing or objective possible. What makes everything possible is experience and expertise. One has to experience, even in the remotest corner of his mind (imagination) and in the deepest chamber of his heart (feelings or emotion), even before experiencing the possibilities of anything in the material plane, the truth and reality of something that one desires to manifest. Only then can one make everything possible.

Can you imagine vividly and can you convince yourself by experiencing everything involved in being a doctor who is married to the most beautiful and loving woman of your dreams? If you do, then it is as good as you've already got it. Can't see it? Can't experience it? Can't believe it? All you do is to train and discipline yourself into becoming a deserving person, a person who deserves everything good in this life, that something you consider good and seeing yourself having it, living it even in your imagination. Once you are convinced that you deserve the best in life, not only because you have done good things in life or that you have never done anything wrong, but most of all because you are convinced in the deepest sense that you deserve everything good regardless of anything else. You deserve just because you live your natural you.

Everything is possible for those who can experience even in their imagination those things they desire to be, to do, and to have in his life. Experience it, imagine it, and have fun.

How to Create a Lasting Personal Happiness

03/22/17

GIVEN THAT THE PREMISE "THE only way to enjoy lasting happiness is to live the life you personally created for yourself…" is true, I created some suggestions on how this works on the individual level. This idea is an abstract from the indisputable fact that everything that exists, both natural and man-made, is the solidification and function of a creative mind. I personally applied this method to myself and found it to be very effective. I just want to share my experience. Who knows, it may also work for you.

1. Discover those things—types of people and relationships, events, and activities—that lift up your spirit or that excites you naturally.
2. Make a list of at least ten items in each category of the ones mentioned above.
3. Rank and prioritize the items on your list, starting from highest priority down to the least.
4. Pick one from each category, the ones that dominate most of your thoughts and feelings in almost all your present moments.

I could add a hundred more items to the list, but for the purpose of just showing an example, I picked only four items to work on.

An Example of Discovering Myself

After mentally revisiting my past concerning those "happy moments" of my life, I decided on the following as among the ones that make me smile just by thinking of them.

Activity 1: List ten things I love to do

1. Creating my paper houses and other handicrafts, such as crocheting, sewing, embroidery

2. Writing down my true feelings in a given moment, maybe a story, a beautiful experience, or a dream or aspiration

3. Listening to wholesome and favorite music, singing, composing lyrics of a song, dancing alone or with a group of good friends

4. Drawing or sketching or painting

5. Socializing, speaking, or being surrounded by an audience of wholesome, attentive, and appreciative people

6. Visiting and exercising or doing physical activities such as calisthenics in the gym

7. Swimming in a pool or a river or the beach

8. Taking photographs of natural beauties, innocent babies, flowers, and many things that I perceive as beautiful and worth preserving

9. Hiking or walking in parks, next to highways, and most especially by a beautiful riverbanks, or a cool mountaintop that overlooks a village, looking at blossoming wild flowers in a wide green meadow at a valley or plateau, and walking by the beach

10. Pedaling a bike around a wholesome and opulent subdivision

Activity 2: list ten types of people and relationships that lift my spirit

1. My son and his beautiful children

2. My daughter and her lovely family

3. My husband

4. My best friend

5. Seeing old friends like Mina, Becky, Betty, Fredy, Raul Escobar, Ronald, Neneng

6. My dad and mom

7. My sister and brother with their families

8. Some of my favorite ex-colleagues like Nayding, Odette, Ma'am Grace, Ma'am Shirley, Ma'am Orfi, and new acquaintances they introduce to me

9. My cousins Selfa and Silvici

10. My biological mother, Esperanza

There could be more listed, such as job, education, career, leisure, and travels. The idea is you should recall all those things, people, events, places, and things that you possess and that actually make you happy in the past and present and you sure will also be in your future.

Now, using the two categories in the example above:

For the first category, I take number 5 as the number one in the rank, and this is what I strongly feel as my immediate need. "Socializing, speaking, or being surrounded by an audience of wholesome, attentive, happy, appreciative, and inspiring people."

Then my next choice to rank number one in the next category should jibe with my rank one in the first category, so I pick number 8. In this I realize that my immediate need is a career similar to what I had when

I was with them that could uplift my spirit. Or, it could be that I need to have a job again in another setting and that my happiness would be when I socialize with wholesome people in a wholesome setting.

Realizing this particular need in a given time, then I would know what to do. Following are some possibilities:

1. Contact my daughter or Ma'am Veron, my best friend, or any close friend within my proximity

2. Arrange a party and tell them to invite their friends

3. Create a viable reason for the party, something that convinced them of your being an attractive, if not irresistible, friend

4. Prepare an agenda to make the party alive

This party may be free, sponsored, or you spend for everything. The idea is to discover your immediate need and create a situation to meet such a need. Don't include financial problems in planning a situation like this; you will be surprised that ideas and resources present themselves once your mind is made up.

There could be more activities while alone working on your favorite hobbies, such as drawing or sketching and painting or creating some handicrafts that you enjoy doing.

Okay. That's all for now. Good luck! Fill your days with happiness. Work for it.